Will suit fit?

Mathematical problem-solving with children

Dora Whittaker

The right of the University of Cambridge to print and sell all manner of books was granted by Henry VIII in 1534. The University has printed and published continuously since 1584.

CAMBRIDGE UNIVERSITY PRESS
Cambridge
London New York New Rochelle
Melbourne Sydney

Published by the Press Syndicate of the University of Cambridge
The Pitt Building, Trumpington Street, Cambridge CB2 1RP
32 East 57th Street, New York, NY 10022, USA
10 Stamford Road, Oakleigh, Melbourne 3166, Australia

First published 1986

Printed in Great Britain at the University Press, Cambridge

Phototypesetting and diagrams by
Gecko Limited, Bicester, Oxon.

British Library Cataloguing in Publication Data
Whittaker, Dora
Will Gulliver's suit fit?:
mathematical problem-solving with children.
1. Problem solving 2. Mathematics—Problems, exercises, etc.
I. Title
510 QA63

Library of Congress Cataloging-in-Publication Data
Whittaker, Dora.
Will Gulliver's suit fit?
1. Problem solving. 2. Mathematics—Study and
teaching (Elementary) I. Title
QA63.W47 1986 372.7 85-19029

ISBN 0 521 31490 9

Contents

Introduction

Mathematics is a stiff discipline. It is also part of the compulsory curriculum, which means that many teachers whose strengths lie in other areas have to teach it. In my inservice courses, both in Britain and in America, I have worked with non-specialists in mathematics, and with specialists. This has proved to be an ideal situation for promoting frank discussions on the significance of a mathematical concept and its relevance in the structure of the subject, and on learning processes which can further understanding. Substantiation of the opinions offered came from teachers' own classrooms: age range of children from entrants to secondary, and variations in ability from the most able to the less able. It is upon these actual examples of children's work and my own that I base this commentary. Thus, though opinions offered are debatable, the substance upon which they are based is irrefutable. It happened!

My main concern is an investigation into how children reason in a *problem-solving* situation and, in context, the bearing this may have on *problem-posing* (a major concern today). Problem-solving as a reasoning activity is much in mind in present educational programmes. The American *An Agenda for Action* (National Council of Teachers of Mathematics) name it as the focus for the present decade, while in the document *Monitoring Mathematics* (Assessment of Performance Unit (A.P.U.), Department of Education and Science, London), it is described as 'a recognised objective in mathematics learning'. The function of problem-solving as defined in both documents goes far deeper than the common interpretation, namely 'to give the answer'. The latter report, for example, defines it as a reasoning process requiring 'to hold in mind a number of possibilities without settling for one immediately'. I read this as a progression from what is known to *a* conclusion: not necessarily the one a book and/or teacher, or indeed computer program, has decided is *the* conclusion (a sure way to neutralise creative thinking).

What type of learning is conducive to this activity? A distinction is made in the A.P.U. document between two types of learning: relational and instrumental. It states, 'While instrumental learning can promote short-termed effectiveness in that processes are carried out properly to produce a "correct" result, understanding mathematics relationally is more satisfying in the long-term, because unifying structures form the conceptual basis for further learning'. It is upon relational learning that I shall be concentrating. Such learning provides the setting for the exercise of logical reasoning which, in turn, is the main activity in problem-solving. Problems need to be posed with this in mind, to give children the opportunity to reason.

Now to an intrinsic element in this form of learning, namely the building of relationships and unifying structures. To embrace it I offer, through exercises in classification (Chapter 2), an approach that has proved practical in awakening children's awareness of relationships and promoting its growth. A study of their reactions reveals how such understanding is furthered by crossing subject barriers, indeed how freeing the process from a purely mathematical context gives children a sounder basis for understanding. One could describe this as a form of purposeful 'integration', not of subject matter *per se* as in projects, but of learning processes. This is not an unnatural transition: problem-solving based on related factors is customary practice be it in subject areas, or indeed in personal and social life.

Back to mathematics! Here I would suggest, as an educator, that no greater disservice could be done to those in our care than to side-step problem-solving in mathematics and settle for memorisation of procedures. To neglect so fertile a field for promotion of logical thinking would be to me, a farmer's daughter, as mad as letting the richest land go fallow.

And finally what areas are in mind for this cultivation of a reasoning approach? I quote those listed in the A.P.U. pamphlet in the context of the activity of problem-solving, namely: concepts; skills and their application; generalisation and proof; and investigations and creativity.

Influenced by the aforementioned factors, and happily enriched by my bank of actual examples of children's reasoning, I propose making my approach to relational learning on two main fronts:

(1) the mental processes involved and, in context,
(2) the special attributes of mathematics which are conducive to the application of these processes, namely its interrelationships and structure.

This study, on the two related fronts, provides the setting for consideration of factors that influence *problem-solving* and thus inevitably those that affect *problem-posing and selection*. As a child depends upon the universal requisite, namely knowledge of background factors which can be related, as a basis for the search for a solution, so problems need to be posed or selected in this context.

Overview of my approach

(This is based on the approach used in my inservice courses.)

Format of chapters

Each of the chapters consists of a discussion on the particular topic to be investigated, followed by examples of children's work to illustrate their reactions (which may be expected or unexpected!). Further discussion based on these reactions (describing how they lead on to consequent stages of development), and opinions of leading educators, are offered where these are pertinent.

Areas under consideration

The areas of mathematics being considered are those listed in the A.P.U. pamphlet *Monitoring Mathematics*. They are:

- *concepts*, where activities are offered which can promote understanding;
- *skills and their application*, where examples are given to illustrate respective functions of each skill with emphasis on logical progression (as opposed to learning 'gimmick' rules);
- *generalisation and proof* and *investigations and creativity*, where examples are offered in context as they arise naturally during the activities.

Analysis of chapters

Chapters 1 and 2 (introduction). These illustrate practical means to meet children's needs in an approach based on reasoning, with emphasis on means for assessing stages of development. Chapter 1 shows ways of analysing children's abilities to make logical deductions. Chapter 2 offers a guide to stages in reasoning capability based on the degree of competence used when classifying in increasingly complex situations. Based on this guide, a framework for primary mathematics is offered (see the Note overleaf).

Chapters 3–7 (core topics). Chapter 3 illustrates ways to help young children understand basic concepts, for example number and (later) order, in limited situations by matching and comparing. The ability to order influences progress in the topics covered in subsequent chapters. Chapter 4 relates number to units of measurement which leads on to numerical differences and ordering. Chapter 5 relates numbers to form ordered pairs as in multiplication tables, and illustrates how the laws of arithmetic can affect such pairing and provide labour-saving practices. Chapter 6 relates these ordered pairs to graphical representations. Chapter 7 investigates angles in the context of symmetrical properties of regular polygons, and similar triangles as they arose in graphs in Chapter 6, and proceeds to angles of elevation in height finding.

Chapter 8 (creative reasoning). This chapter discusses examples of creative work by pupils of initiative, as they evolved during class sessions, and also developed from them as individual logical progressions.

The appendix (notation). This describes stages of reasoning as they arise working in base 10, and the extension via pattern to other bases, with particular attention paid to base 2.

Note: For a syllabus which relates to these chapters, see page 20.

1 Examples of children's reasoning

My main theme in the chapters which follow will be a consideration of children's ability to make logical deductions within the framework of mathematical structure. As an introduction, I offer here examples withdrawn from that context so that factors influencing children's ability to reach true conclusions can be studied independently. It may be of immediate relief to teachers to know that where any seemingly odd conclusion is reached it does not, *ipso facto*, spring from faulty teaching.

Firstly, what factors should be considered when making an analysis of children's reasoning? In reply I quote this definition of logical deduction as proffered in *LOGIC* (Nuffield Mathematical Project):

This is the reasoning process by which, starting from some initial statement or statements (often called premisses), we are led to one or more conclusions. If the reasoning is carried out properly, we may call the process a 'valid argument', and the validity of the argument is entirely independent of whether the premisses are in fact true or not. If they are true, a valid argument of course leads to a true conclusion . . . it is very desirable for teachers always to bear in mind the distinction between the correctness or validity of reasoning and the truth of the conclusions reached.

In short, we should investigate the following when analysing children's reasoning.

(1) *The premiss or premisses upon which the argument is based. Are they true or false?*

(2) *The argument. Is it valid or not?*

A true conclusion depends upon a valid argument based on true premisses. A false conclusion may be the result of false reasoning or false premisses. It is on this basis that the following examples of children's reasoning should be analysed. On the assumption that you will prefer to conduct your own analysis, I offer personal comments only where they may be relevant.

Setting: Florida (pupils aged 5–6 years)

I had been invited by the teacher to join in her effort, as a preliminary to teaching measurement, to define 'bigger than'/'smaller than' when making comparisons of size. According to the best canons of 'pedagogy', I produced a model by standing (all 4 feet $11\frac{1}{2}$ inches of me!) at the side of their expectedly taller teacher and asked, "How do I compare with your teacher?". Before anyone could answer, a little lad dashed protectively forward, glared threateningly at the others and said "Don't say it – she can't help it – they have to be little where she comes from so that they can all get on her little island." Be kind in your analysis of my Sir Galahad!

Of interest and relevance here, but of linguistic rather than mathematical import, I met an even more surprising conjecture from American students who were 16 years old. At the end of a session which I had taken, students were invited to ask questions. One girl asked, "Would you please speak English?". I was embarrassed for her until the consultant who had brought me asked who else would like to hear me speak English – result, a full show of hands. What premisses would you attribute to the conclusion which caused this request?

Setting: English junior school (first-year less-able pupils)

A teacher with a most sensitive rapport with these pupils had given them wide experience in fitting string across a diameter of a circle, then around its circumference, or along the distance travelled in one complete turn. Finally the conclusion was reached that a circumference is just over three times a diameter. Then the great moment arrived. The Head Teacher was escorted to his car by the pupils with the promise that they could tell him how far his car travelled with one turn of the wheels, without him even having to drive it. One group moved across to a wheel, measured the diameter of the wheel and painstakingly multiplied the result by 3, giving an answer of just over 180 cm. The teacher beamed with pride! Then, to her surprise and chagrin, other groups moved to the other wheels and repeated the process. Answers were compared, then one set proclaimed with great pride, "Ours is the best wheel Sir – it takes you further than all the others." Proof, if proof is needed in our profession, that, quoting Burns, 'the best laid schemes o' mice an' men – gang aft a-gley'.

Setting: English secondary school (second-year pupils)

The Head of the Mathematics Department, as a means for monitoring pupils' understanding of the concept of area, posed the problem of finding the area of an unusual shape of their own choice. He forwarded the contribution shown in Fig. 1.1 to me with his 'warmest regards'. (Of interest, the same glib response as Peter's to a definition of area was given by 90% of adults in a consequent survey.)

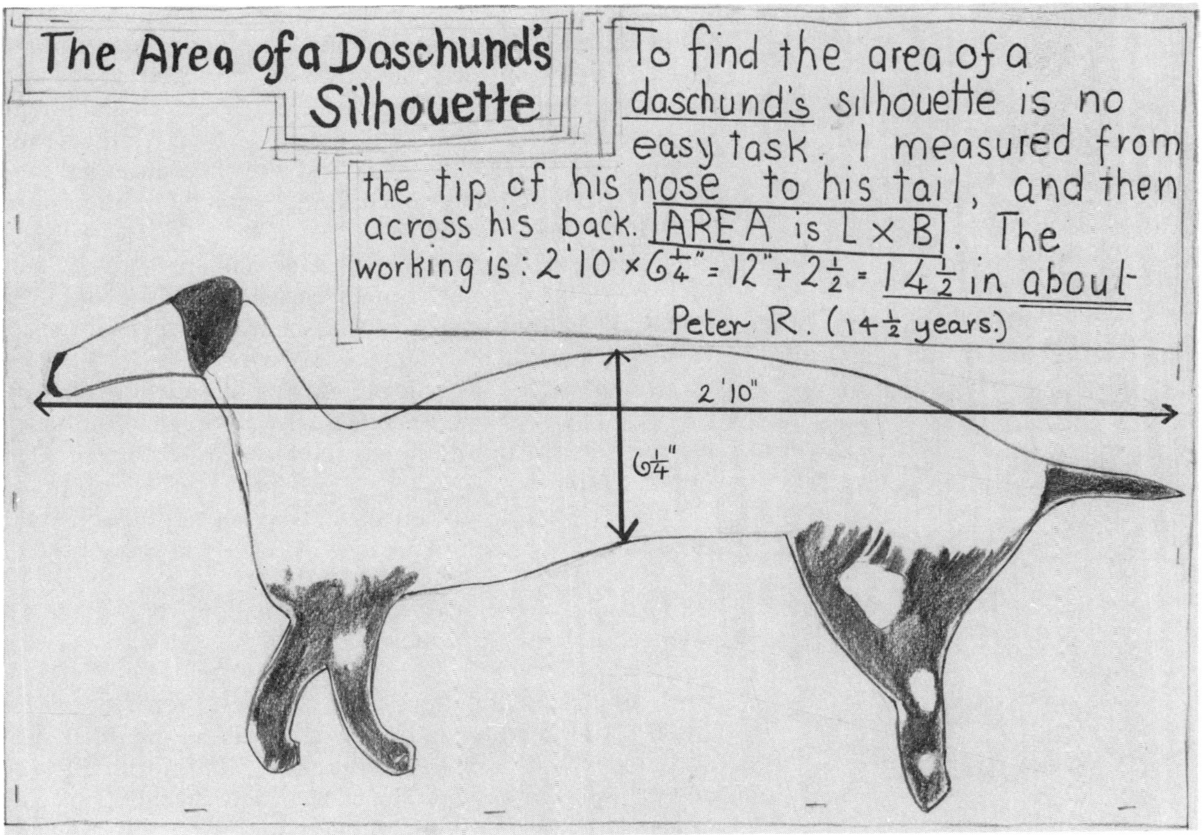

Fig. 1.1

On enquiry Peter's method of calculating was found to be created by himself to meet the need of the moment. It is worth analysing!

Obviously the premiss is 'inappropriate'. But how do you rank the argument itself?

Setting: English junior school (pupils aged 7–8 years, varying ability)

The preceding examples illustrate a practical matter of professional concern namely that, even among pupils of the same age, there exists inevitably a wide range of abilities. In the Cockcroft Report *Mathematics counts,* commissioned in Britain, the committee reports a seven year gap in the achievements of children in mathematics – an example quoted could be answered at the age of 10 years but not at 11 years, further some 14 year olds could not answer it but some 7 year olds could. Professor Cockcroft's own comment, as quoted in a Press report, was as follows: 'the change [in mathematics syllabuses] must start by recognising the difference in ability right across an age-range; examining bodies and teacher trainers will need to combine'. This implies a concerted effort to meet natural discrepancies.

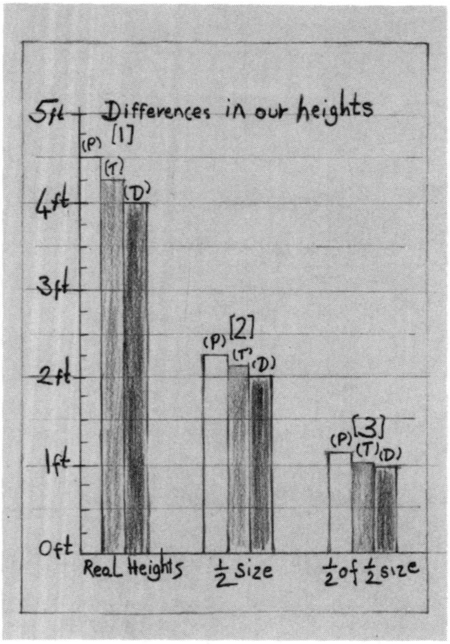

Fig. 1.2

I now offer an example illustrating three widely different levels of reasoning, based on the reactions of three pupils (aged $7\frac{1}{2}$ years) in the same situation.

Dawn, Paul and Tim had constructed a block graph with strips to represent their *real* heights when I joined their group. Their interest was to find the differences in their heights. Questioning revealed that Dawn did not understand 'difference'; the boys did.

I suggested that they now made half-size models, then half-size of these, and so on. The stages are illustrated in Fig. 1.2 as far as quarter-size, obviously reduced here for space reasons. They halved again (not shown here).

Dawn thoroughly enjoyed halving her previous strips as instructed by the boys, became totally absorbed in the activity, particularly sticking down the strips as instructed. Hers not to reason why.

Now to the discussion on differences as shown by the strips, and the reasoning evoked by each pupil:

Dawn had moved forward a step. She pointed to graph [1] saying, "It shows our differences."

Paul, understanding the halving process, realised that as graph [2] represented half their real sizes so the differences appeared as half their real differences. Then turning to [3], and [4] (not shown here), he added, "See, the differences are disappearing – soon there will be none."

Tim understood completely. In reply to the question, "If you kept on halving and halving again, would the differences not be there?", he replied, "No, they would look as if they'd gone but they wouldn't. We are not the same so there will always be differences." Deep thought, then a relieved smile spread over his face, "If you halve the strips you just halve the differences – they keep halving when the strips do. Halve and halve the strips for ever, you just halve and halve the differences for ever – it never ends but it's there."

What is your opinion of each one's ability to reason? (The concept of ratio will evolve again in the David/Goliath example (page 35), and in the Gulliver/Lilliputian project (page 57).)

On practical grounds, I would suggest that group work such as the above is an invaluable source for assessment. To a watching listening teacher (when time allows this), strengths and weaknesses in pupils' abilities to reason surface naturally during discussions with their peers. There is no incentive here to give the expected answer as there often is in adult 'interviewing'.

2 Stages in reasoning

Problem-solving in mathematics requires not only a knowledge of certain concepts and skills but also, as noted in the American *Agenda for Action*, 'of the relationships among them, and the fundamental principles that unify them'. This awareness can be likened to that of a railway complex: a review of the linkage between the several branches can lead to an appreciation of its overall structure. Further, just as such appreciation grows only gradually and through experience, so in mathematics an awareness of inter-relationships leading to structure is only slowly progressive. Piaget describes the process as, 'a spontaneous and gradual construction of mathematical structures [which] exist as a function of intelligence'.

As a pre-study of factors that can influence pupils' reactions to relationships, and their conclusions, I offer examples which have arisen when children are required to match and compare, as in classification. The factors that influence them can then be investigated, and later form a basis for appraisal of related experiences as they arise in the more specific arithmetical and/or geometrical branches of mathematics which follow. Factors worthy of note are the influence of age/maturity, and pre-conditioning to finding relationships – with particular reference to the number of attributes that can be dealt with, for example 6 as a multiple of 2 (only) or 6 as a multiple of 3 (only) or then onto 6 as a multiple of both 2 and 3.

Classification

Classification, viewed in this light, serves two main educational purposes:

(a) *on a child level it provides an activity which helps to establish relationships;*

(b) *on a teacher level it offers means for assessing the stage reached in a child's knowledge and reasoning ability.*

The examples of children's reactions to classification should provide a basis for your appraisal of these claims. In classification the different relationships are represented as follows.

Fig. 2.1 Disjoint sets

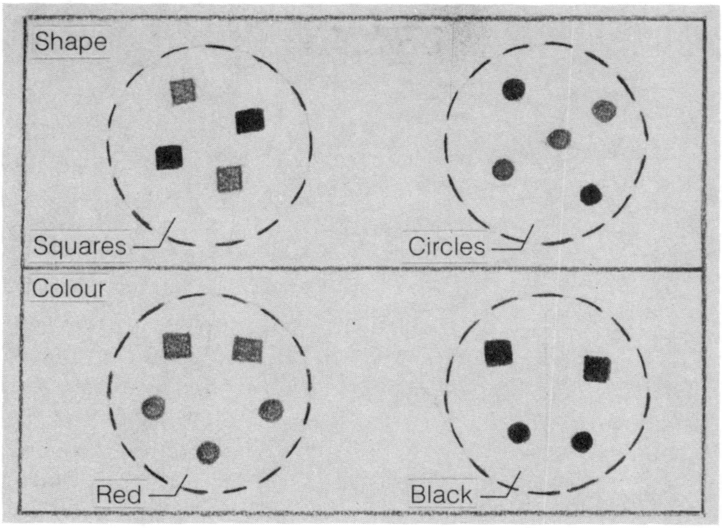

(1) *Disjoint sets:* separate sets for each attribute, as for {boys}/{girls}.
(2) *Inclusion:* one set contained within another, as for {boys}/ {children}.
(3) *Intersection:* one set overlapping another, as for {multiples of 2}/{multiples of 3}, where 6 belongs to the intersection.

Note: set (Venn) diagrams are used as tools for representing classifications. The main concern, however, must be for the truth of the premiss(es) upon which the classifications are made.

On the practical front, note from the examples which follow the crossing of subject barriers to provide additional experience, the lead into more precise use of language (for example 'both', 'and'), and the use of hoops and three-dimensional material, particularly with young children, because moveable objects allow for an easy change of attribute for consideration (as in Fig. 2.1).

We shall now consider the three relationships above in turn, and so illustrate the stages in reasoning. (Note: for the *union* of two sets, see page 19.)

Disjoint sets

Sorting is such a common activity with young children that opportunities are manifold. If three-dimensional objects and hoops are used, these can be moved when re-thinking occurs, as in Fig. 2.1 (where there was a change of attribute from shape to colour).

One example that was pictorially very interesting was when a class drew themselves in seven separate sets based on the rhyme 'Monday's child is fair of face, Tuesday's child is full of grace, . . .'. Day of birth, not physical attribute, determined the sets.

Main categories are easily classified, for example: in mathematics, shapes or odd/even numbers; and, in biology, say vertebrates/invertebrates. With live creatures, criteria for differentiation can prove debatable, as one finds in classifying children. (I have noted a problem posed in a computer program on such arguable attributes as red hair, fat-faced and big feet.) A similar problem faced Brian when he sought to classify a dozen birds according to size and shape of beak, and then match types with the kind of food they ate. Examples were:

short/thick beak	e.g. finch/insect eaters
sifting beak	e.g. swan/grub eaters
sharp/hooked beak	e.g. vulture/flesh eaters
serrated beak	e.g. toucan/fruit eaters.

At least the birds did not argue the point!

Many examples of disjoint sets occur in the rest of this book, not represented by diagrams as here, but visualised mentally as on an adult level.

Inclusion

Young children find this 'part/whole' or 'some/all' relationship difficult. A helpful idea is to place a small hoop inside a large one, with the large one labelled, for example, TOYS, and the inside one, say, DOLLS or MODEL CARS.

This can lead to an understanding that (say) dolls are toys, but not all toys are dolls. Similarly all squares are rectangles, but not all rectangles are squares. Take the arithmetical example shown in Fig. 2.2. Set *B* is the numbers between 1 and 9, that is 2, 3, 4, 5, 6, 7, 8. Set *A* is the even numbers between 1 and 9, that is 2, 4, 6, 8. *A* is included in *B*, which is written in mathematical notation as $A \subset B$.

Fig. 2.3 shows a biological example of set inclusion (used with girls aged 9 years). Other examples of inclusion in the set of mammals (used with the same group of pupils) were:

Fig. 2.2

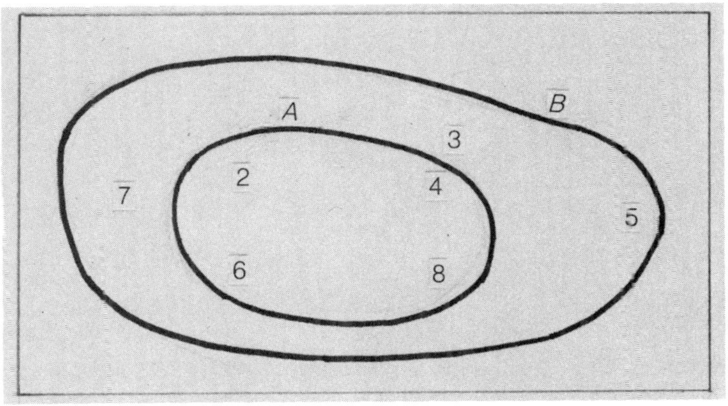

Fig. 2.3

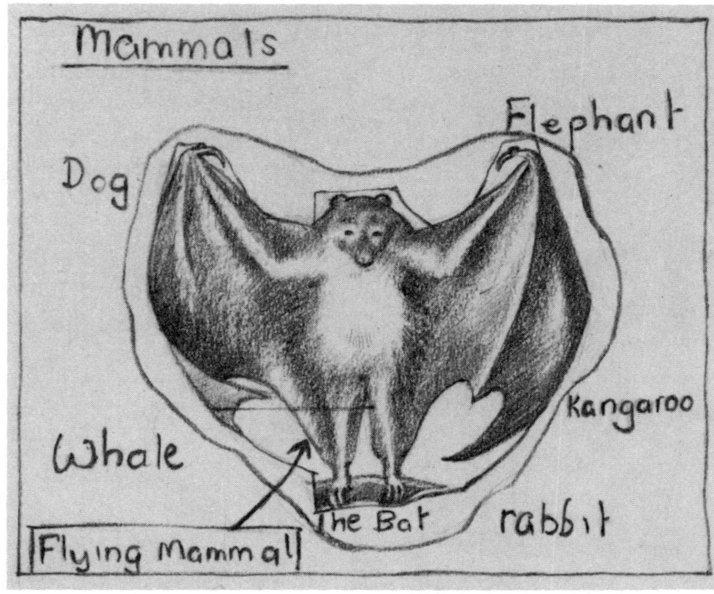

those that lay eggs (echidna, platypus) and marsupials (kangaroo, opossum).

A group of boys investigated metals, for example {iron objects}/{those that cut}.

Intersection

This is even more difficult for young children than inclusion, as it entails dealing with partial overlap of more than one attribute: in this example {children with brothers}/ {children with sisters}.

The Venn diagram in Fig. 2.4 illustrates the four possible categories.

(1) *a* but not *b* (children with sisters but not brothers).
(2) *b* but not *a* (children with brothers but not sisters).
(3) both *a* and *b* (children with *both* brothers *and* sisters).
(4) neither *a* nor *b* (children with *neither* brothers *nor* sisters).

Fig. 2.4

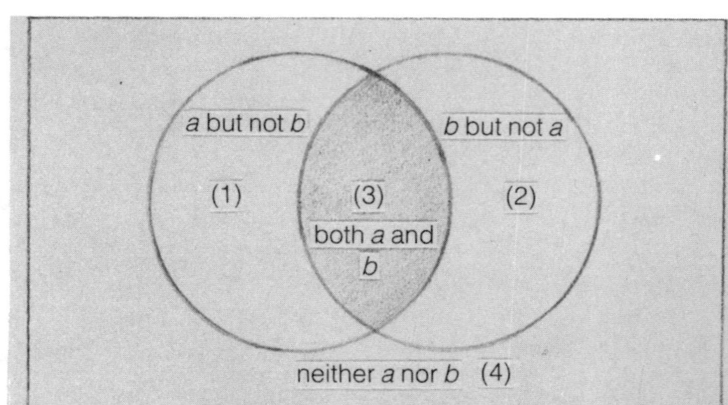

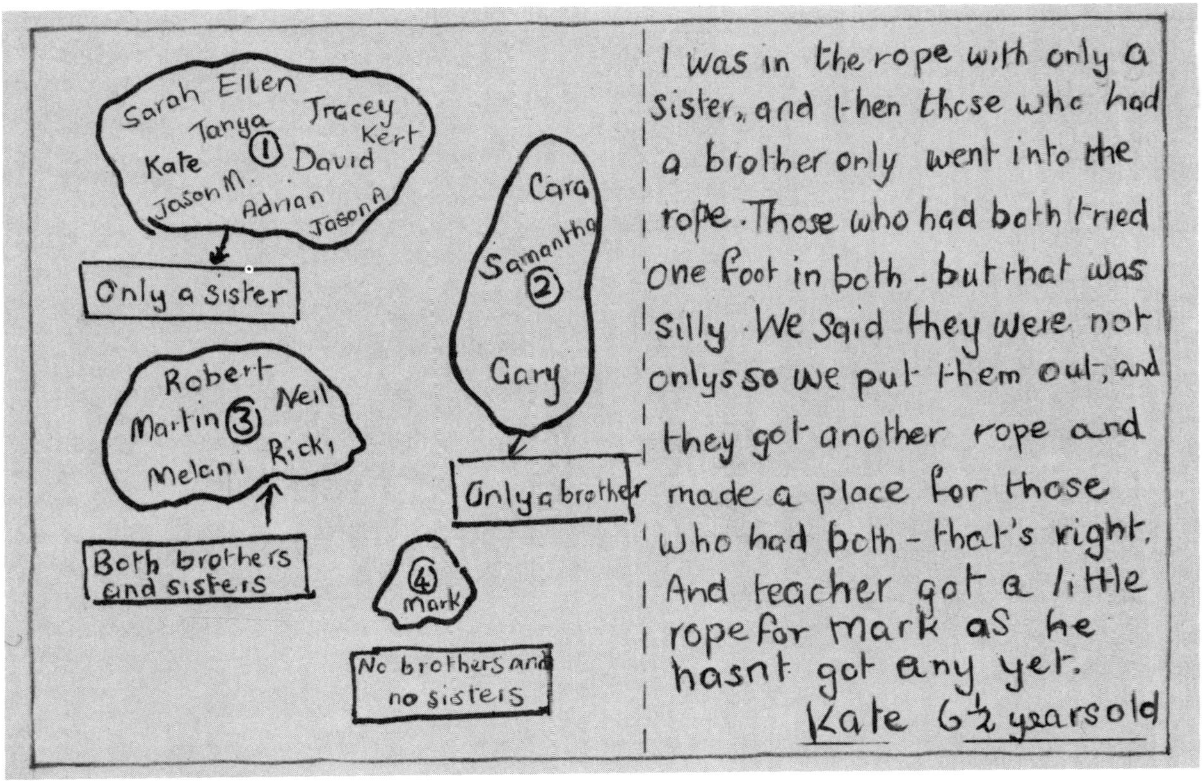

Fig. 2.5

Fig. 2.5 shows what actually happened on this brother/ sister problem when it was used with a class of six year olds. It is an illustration of a pre-Venn diagram.

Now let us turn to mathematical and biological examples from older children (girls aged 9 years). The example in Fig. 2.6 is offered as it caused considerable controversy. All agreed that 2 was an even number, but only Jill said it was also a prime number. She used a model of Eratosthenes sieve to prove her point.

Fig. 2.6

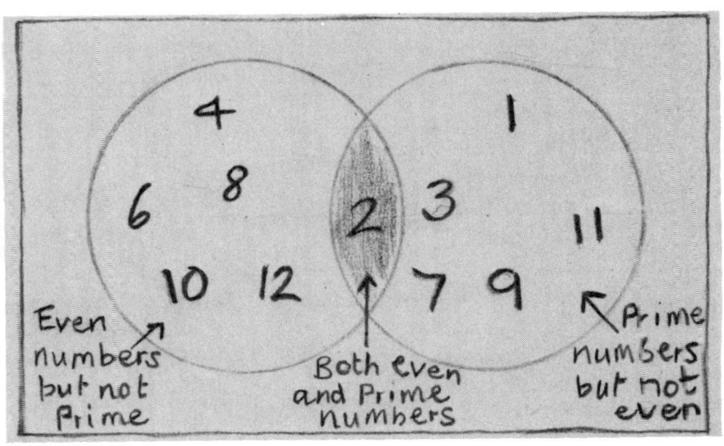

The following biological examples were also discovered and illustrated.

Fish (habitat): (a) sea water, (b) fresh water, both (a) and (b).
Mammals (habitat): (a) sea, (b) land, both (a) and (b).
Mammals (food): (a) herbivores, (b) carnivores, both (a) and (b).

Lastly, here are mathematical examples from two pupils (aged 11 years) with comments attached.

Fig. 2.7 (top)

Fig. 2.8 (bottom)

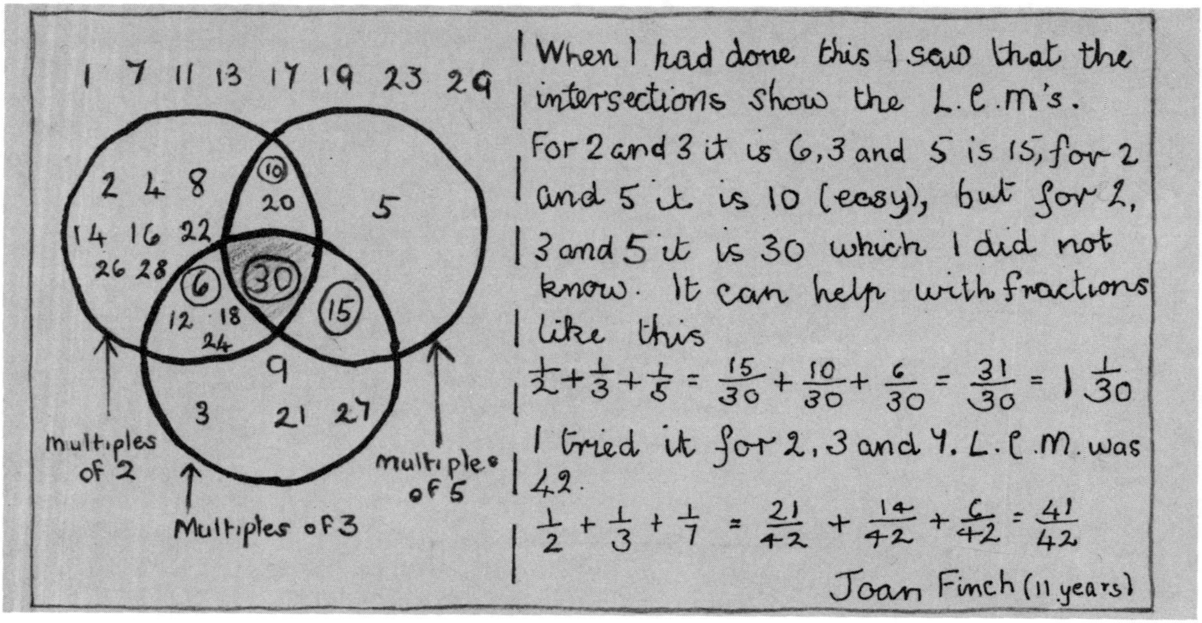

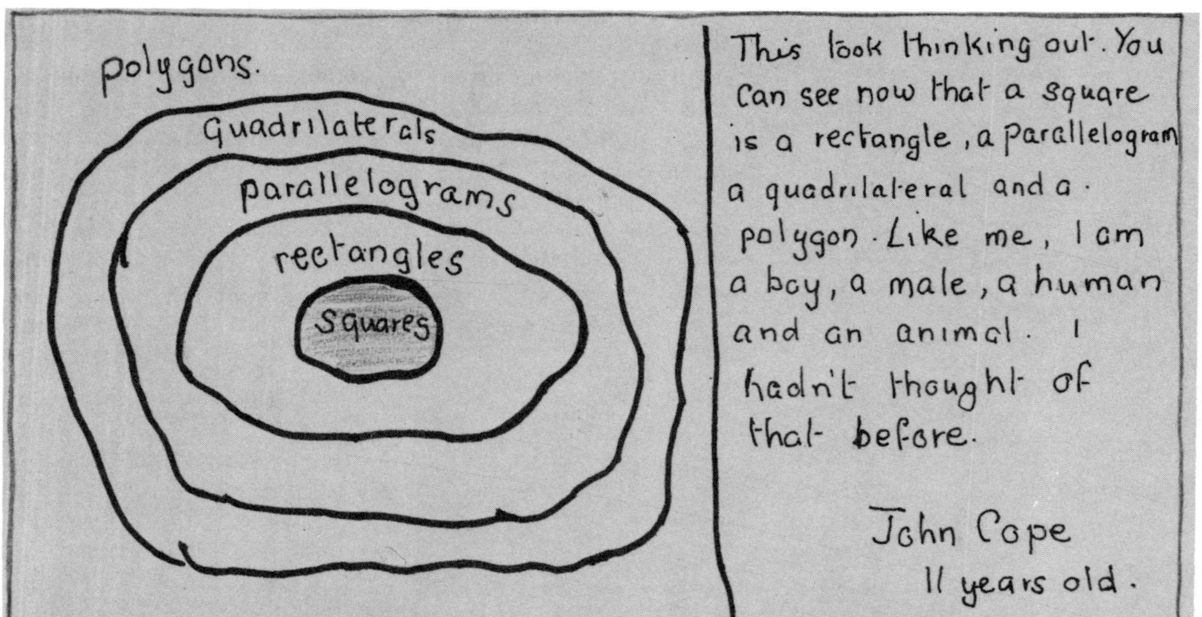

Fig. 2.9

The following incident is of interest as an illustration of the reaction of a parent. I was once invited to speak at a parent's evening in a university area. A professor of mathematics at the university remarked, "I came prepared to shoot on hearing from my daughter (aged $7\frac{1}{2}$ years) about hoops, hoops and hoops again . . . (supportive noises!) Not now – this is sheer basic mathematical experience. What about a course for fathers?"

I cannot leave these forms of representation of relationships without referring to the *union* (putting together) *of two sets*. As a physical operation it is a common practice with all ages, yet its importance with young children may easily be overlooked unless it is realised that it offers basic experience leading to the mental abstract operation of addition where the symbol + (plus) is used. Fig. 2.9 is an example using cardinal numbers to express the numerical property of the separate sets and their union.

A framework for primary mathematics

After this exemplification of growth through extension of awareness of relationships and the ability to deal with them, there follows a chart which indicates a similar growth in the numerical and spatial aspects of mathematics with a consequent alignment in approach. It can serve as a reference for the remaining chapters, whether they deal with the aspects singly or together, and provide a basis for forming a unified approach. In support note this opinion:

Today there is only one mathematics, a unified mathematics in which all branches are based on concepts and structures (Fehr)

Page 20 shows such a structure. It can be regarded as a syllabus. Read across for similar levels of experience and down for progression in each aspect.

Note: The broken line across the chart indicates on a *broad* front a partition between experiences in infant school (age 5 to 7+ years) and junior school (age 7+ to 11+ years). Chapter 3 (shaded) centres on an early inter-related approach to number and quantity. Chapters 4, 5, 6 and 7 (numbered) offer logical progressions from early experiences; see the Overview of my approach (page 7). All feed in to provide the background for the creative reasoning in Chapter 8.

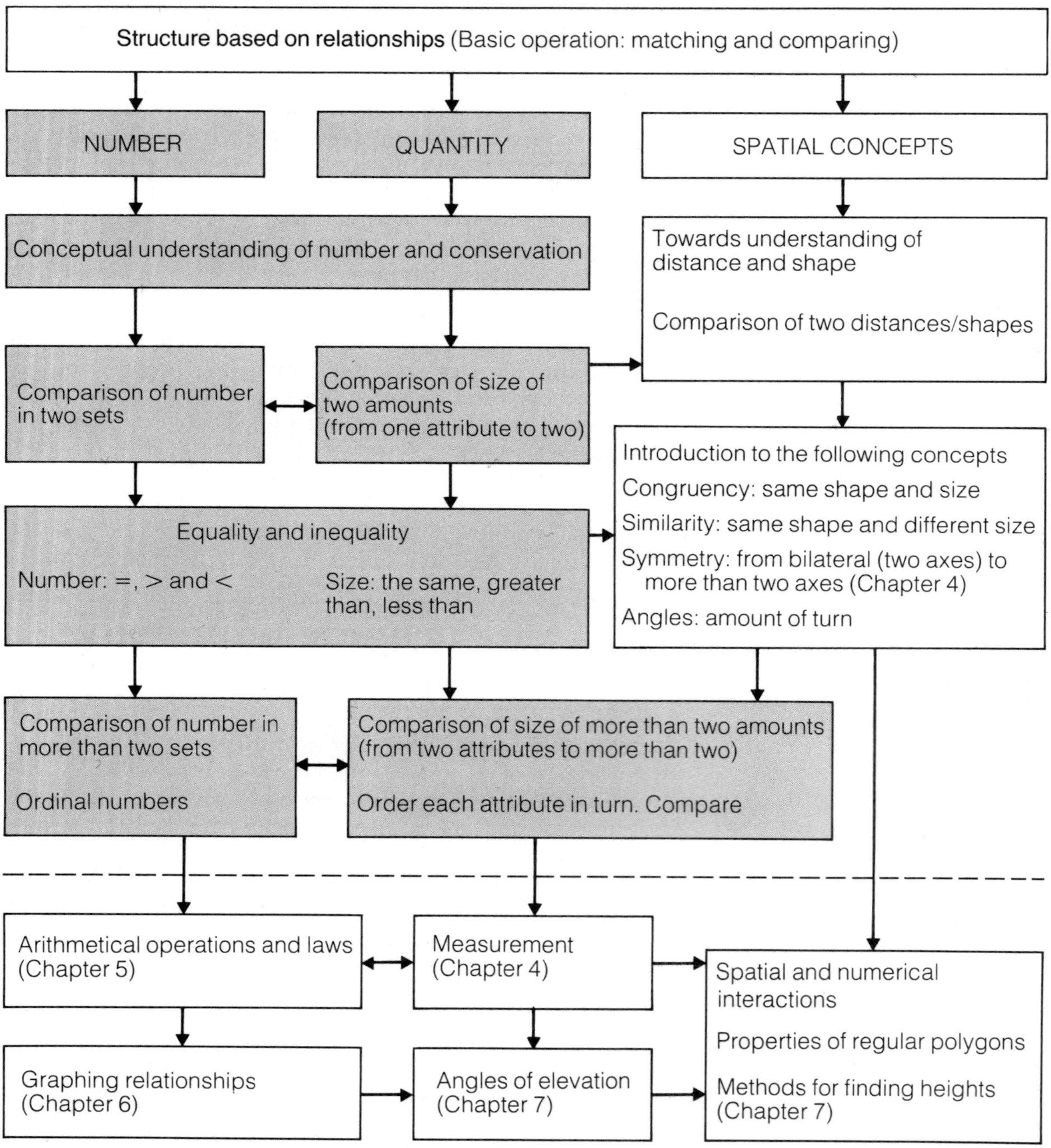

When I move, in Chapters 3–5, to a study of number and quantity and on to the familiar branches of measurement and operations, I follow the same relational approach leading from and into unifying structures. Chapters 6 and 7 on graphs and finding heights just extend the structure. Further, an analysis of the investigations pursued by creative pupils, as offered in Chapter 8, indicates that their thought processes lead them naturally forward along logical lines based on relationships, from conclusion to conclusion. Their reliance on pattern is symptomatic of this approach.

Opinions of this approach

I now list benefits that educators claim can accrue from this form of relational learning. The chapters which follow can then be appraised as a sounding-board for the degree of support such claims merit.

(1) A continuity of mathematical experience, in which ideas already learnt merge into those being learnt, is in line with the process of intellectual development and is therefore natural.

(2) An association of ideas is time-saving; memorisation of facts, for example table facts, is uneconomical and hazardous.

(3) A process in mathematics which aligns growth with an awareness of increasingly complex relationships, provides a fertile field for creative thinking.

I would add, from personal classroom experience, that whatever the age or seeming ability of those pursuing mathematical activities, the difference of approach is in degree not in nature. Whatever the degree, the activity itself takes place within the same structure.

Inter-reaction of problem-posing and problem-solving

This analysis of relational learning has to me, as a teacher, proved akin to trying to explain some seemingly instinctive process. Yet the more conscious awareness of its nature can prove helpful in evaluating problem-solving techniques and, in that context, the factors to be taken into account when posing problems (as noted in the Introduction), be they one's own, those in books or computer programs.

3 Basic experience in number and quantity

Being firmly convinced that relational learning is the operative factor in building a structure for mathematical learning, I requested a move from being a specialist in teaching mathematics with secondary children, first to teaching juniors (aged 7+ to 11+ years), then to infants (aged 5 to 7+ years), to gain first-hand experience of what constitutes this structure. This experience led to the framework offered on page 20. The interest here is with the foundational stage and early experience leading from it.

To provide immediate reference, the relevant section has been extracted from the framework (on page 20). Read down for progression in each aspect, and across for similar levels of experience.

The areas reviewed in this chapter are first the *conceptual understanding of number and conservation*, secondly *comparisons limited to two* (in connection with number and size) and thirdly *comparisons extended to more than two* (in connection with number and size).

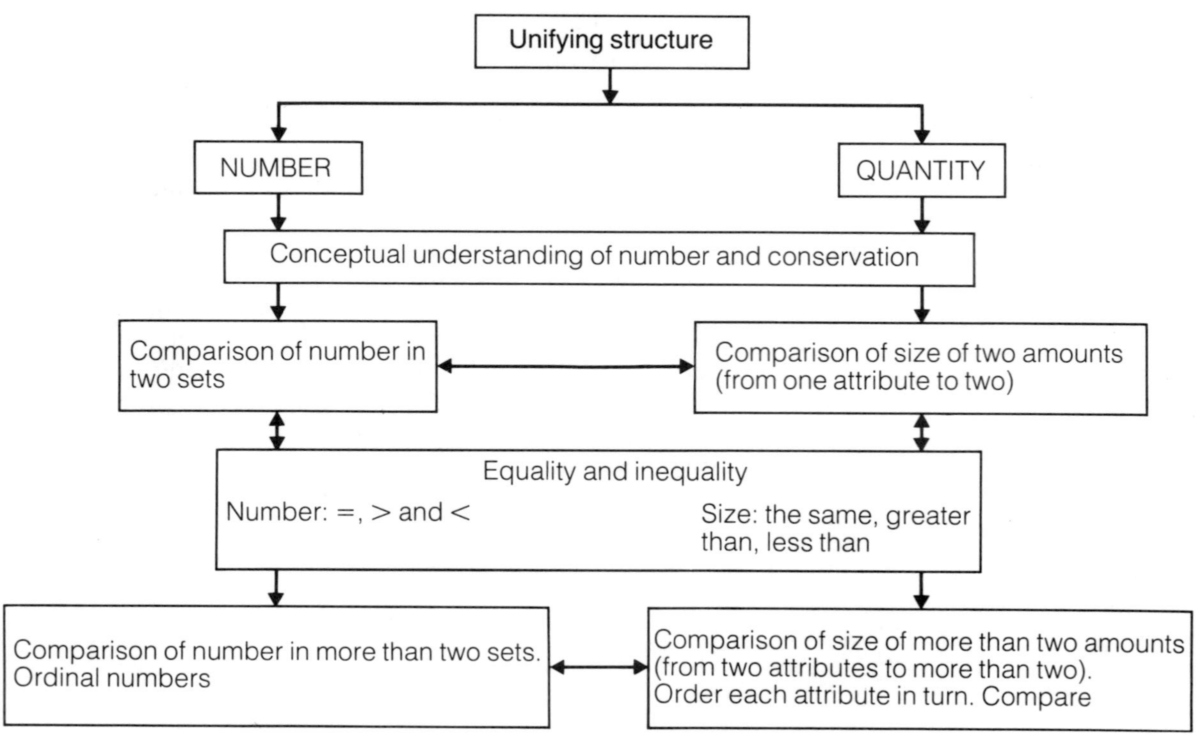

(A digression for a moment from the mathematical to the personal, about when I was taking a class of young children: I refer to the need to be ready for the unexpected. Before reaching school age, Billy was renowned for slipping into school. When he was entered officially, he was put into my class. On the second day he stood up, put his chair back and strode purposefully to the door. His purposefulness alerted me. We met at the door. "Why Billy?" I asked. Said Billy dismissively, "I've had enough". And to this day, when a situation strikes me as too much, I say to myself, "I've had enough".)

As a teacher of all ages, I would like to put on record that teaching young children is no soft option. It requires constant alertness, as shown in the Billy incident, and considerable educational skill, as illustrated later.

Conceptual understanding of number and conservation

Number

A practical point, not always recognised, is that a quantity exists in concrete or fluid form and can be measured, whereas number is an abstraction: a quite fearsome idea when one realises at what a young age children are required to come to terms with it and use it in everyday life. Of it Bertrand Russell writes, 'The number of a set is the class of all sets which can be put into one-to-one correspondence with it. (Two is the class of all pairs and so on) . . . there is no doubt about the class of couples, it is indubitable and not hard to define, whereas the number two, in any other sense, is a metaphysical entity about which we can never feel sure that it exists or that we have tracked it down. There is a distinction between the abstract number two and any set of two things.' In layman's language, two cannot be produced in concrete form, it can only be exemplified by a set of two objects. In practice it is the exemplification, a *one-to-one correspondence*, of objects in equivalent sets that can further understanding, for example fours for appreciation of the fourness of four and so on (one-ness, two-ness and three-ness is generally visibly grasped). Piaget's check-up on the degree of a pupil's understanding of the cardinal (expressing how many) aspect of number is offered in the following section on conservation. How ordering leads to the ordinal aspect is illustrated in Fig. 3.9.

A further practical point concerns the difference in degree of complexity between *understanding* numbers and the mere calligraphy entailed in *writing* the symbols. Fig. 3.1 illustrates the different 'artistic' efforts involved in these

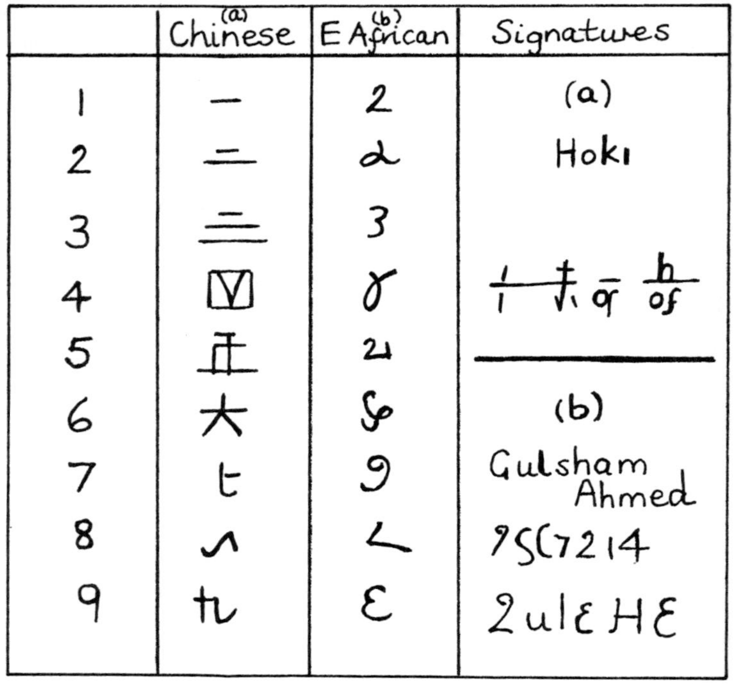

Fig. 3.1 (*Note*: This is my copy of their written efforts – apologies if our combined effort is not truly accurate!)

representations. Hoki and Gulsham attended a school in San Francisco. Their calligraphy was greatly admired. "Just look", said one knowing only the Arabic symbols 1, 2, 3 . . . "they can write theirs as well as ours".

The ability to write symbols, like that of counting as a recitative exercise, does not indicate understanding of number itself.

Conservation

Consider the conservation of number and quantity. Piaget's tests are well known: on number, on liquids (same amount in two identical containers then one poured into another with a different base), on length, on area and so on. In stage 1 the children's thinking is dominated by what they see; in stage 2 they may well be confused by what they see and what their nascent reasoning powers suggest; while at stage 3 they are able to rely on their reasoning and realise that, though appearances may differ, the number or quantity remain the same. The test on number, as mentioned in the previous section, is to place a series of objects in one-to-one correspondence with a standard set, then either spread or pile one set of the objects. Their replies to whether there are now the same number indicates which stage (1 to 3) they are in.

No synchronisation with age can be relied upon. In this context I remember a child (aged 5 years) replying somewhat patronisingly to these tests on number and quantity, "The same of course". By chance it was her mother who took me back to my Miami hotel, and when I referred to her

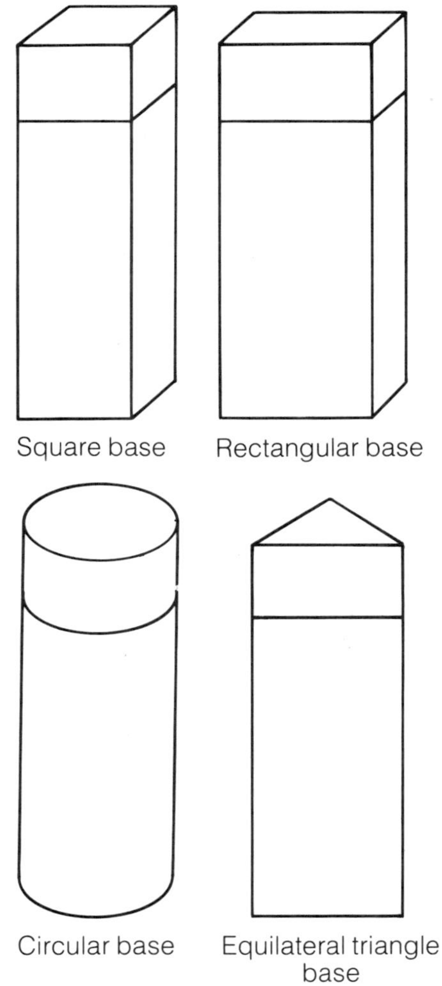

Fig. 3.2 (above)

daughter's unequivocal reaction, she replied, "Well, of course, she is the youngest of five and the only one they trust to share out their candies and drink fairly." On the other hand, consider a boy (aged 9 years) whom the teacher found consistently bashing his lunch-time crisps to fragments. When asked why he did it, he replied, again patronisingly, "You get more that way."

Are we adults, by the way, always conservation-conscious? Obviously the manufacturer thinks not. Note how bottles of expensive perfume or drink are invariably 'flat-faced' with rectangular rather than square or circular bases. The maximum expanse meets the eye! In what order, for example, would you place the containers in Fig. 3.2 for capacity? Would the fact that they have the same height and the same base perimeter change your opinion? If so, what new ordering, if any, do you suggest?

Some secondary boys faced the same problem. Their ordering on sight was (from most to least): rectangular, square, triangular, circular. Awareness that perimeters and heights were the same led them to think the containers might hold the same amount. So they checked by calculating areas of bases which they agreed, after some argument, could be the causal factor, since height would not. Here are the results. In all cases the perimeter was 12 cm and the height was 10 cm.

They drew up a table showing the areas of various rectangles with perimeters 12 cm.

Rectangles (perimeter 12 cm)

Perimeter	2(1 + 5)	2(2 + 4)	2(3 + 3)	2(4 + 2)	2(5 + 1)
Area	5 cm^2	8 cm^2	9 cm^2	8 cm^2	5 cm^2

Fig. 3.3

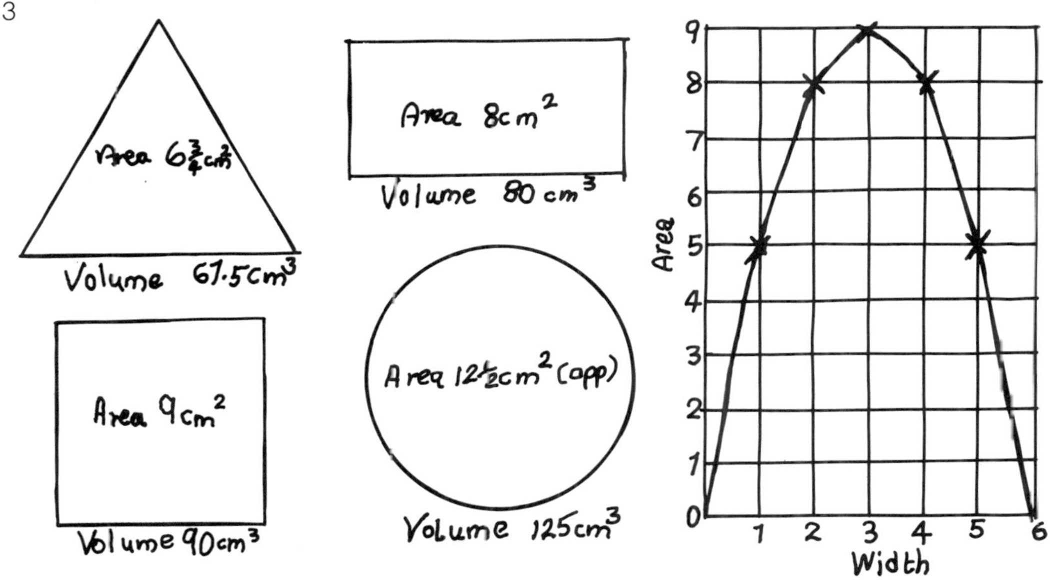

They put the information about areas of rectangles onto a graph (see Fig. 3.3). They also drew sketches of the bases of the various containers.

They concluded that the capacity of the containers, from greatest to least was, circular, square, rectangular, triangular. Their graph illustrated a further factor which was that a narrower rectangular shape (say 5 by 1) could come last and so alter the order of the rectangular and triangular containers. (Personal opinion: good problem, well solved and practical.)

Note: Junior girls (aged 10–11 years) solved the problem by making the four containers in card, standing them in identical saucers, filling them with the *same* substance and weighing them (for an example where there was a different substance see page 32). I like this method.

Comparisons limited to two

As children's understanding of number and size grows, there are, one hopes, some mathematical ideas and language upon which to build. In the early stages, however, the teacher has to use the children's daily experiences and interests as a basis. It is surprising how rich these can prove as a source for promoting reasoning, as the following examples show.

Number (>, <, =)

The 'apparatus' used in this example was the children themselves. It is the work of one group. First the children arranged themselves in sets as shown in Fig. 3.4. Next they stood in one-to-one correspondence ('matching' to them) with each boy paired with a girl.

Fig. 3.4

Boys	Alistair	Matthew	John	Jeremy	Paul
	↓	↓	↓	↓	↓
Girls	Julia	Rachel	Sarah	Tracey	Lisa

This offered an opportunity to check their understanding of equality, and helped to reinforce their awareness of the 'fiveness' of five. Then Jason and Robert joined them, as illustrated later by Tracey and reproduced here in Fig. 3.5. Inequality had replaced equality, and the scene was set for introducing the concepts of *'more than'* and *'less than'*. Consequent discussion seemed to indicate understanding yet, when accounts were written, only Paul Parr (a bystander throughout) referred to the *'less than'* situation. Why? The answer was given to me by Paul when I called in later, *"The less thans aren't there – see, that's why."* A lesson to me from a five-year old!

Fig. 3.5 (above) Fig. 3.6 (below)

The example in Fig. 3.6 shows one-to-one correspondence 'distorted' to suggest equality. John cannily used this, with full awareness, in a good cause (or one that John thought was good!).

At a glance would you think that there were the same number of supporters for Nottingham Forest as Liverpool? If so, that's just what John T., an ardent supporter for Nottingham Forest, and the one trusted to affix the selfportraits, intended. "I spread us out and made me fat enough to fill the row", he whispered to me, "then we look as many as them".

Unfortunately for John, the teacher chose this example to introduce mapping in a non-numerical context (the relation here being 'supports'). When this relation was illustrated as in Fig. 3.7, it could not be mis-read, even by John! However, there was consolation: Nottingham Forest won!

Size (Introduction of attributes)

First note the nascent awareness of certain mathematical principles as exhibited in Paul's artistry (Fig. 3.8). It shows *symmetry* which is reminiscent of ancient artistic drawings; *proportion* in the relative sizes of parts of the body; and *topography* in the relative positioning of parts of the body (no necks, however).

Fig. 3.7

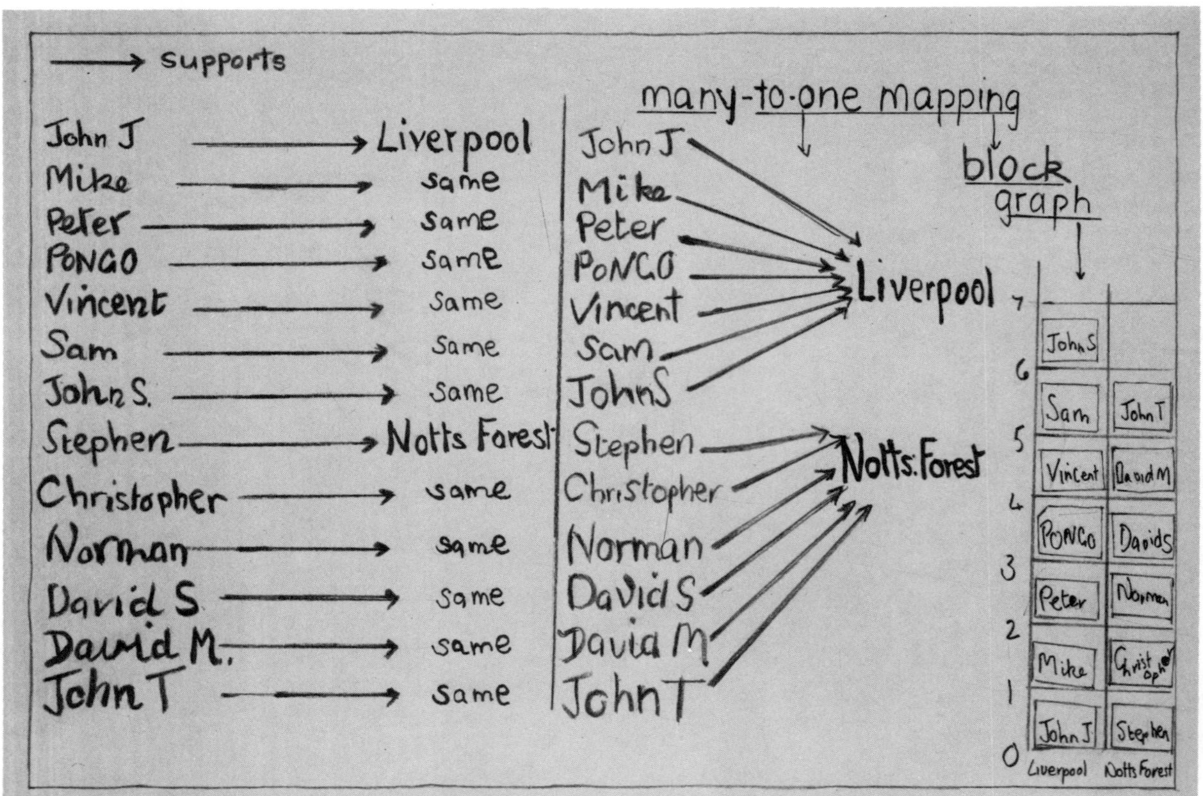

Fig. 3.8

The drawing caused a disagreement. Mark was furious that Paul should think he was 'bigger' than Mark. To illustrate his point, he threw out his arms to show how 'big' *he* was, then almost closed them to indicate Paul's size.

Two inter-related problems surfaced here: firstly the difficulty in dealing with more than one attribute (noted in the section on classification in Chapter 2); and secondly the lack of linguistic ability to describe properly the attribute in mind, i.e. limitation to 'bigger than/smaller than'.

Table 3.1 Relationships based on comparison and matching (see p. 30)

Concept	Non-equality	Equality (conservation)
Size: length	is longer/shorter than	is the same (length) as
height	is taller/shorter than	is the same (height) as
width	is wider/narrower than	is the same (width) as
thickness	is thicker/thinner than	is the same (thickness) as
(also capacity, mass, time, etc.)		
Number	is greater than (>) is less than (<)	is equal to (=)

To meet these problems, the teacher used selected pairs of children as 'models', each centred on an attribute of 'size', then (according to attribute) discussed with the pupils relevant language. Table 3.1 contains a selection of words offered. The addition of number is mine, as it illustrates the complementary nature of geometrical and arithmetical comparisons.

And now back to Mark and Paul's disagreement which led up to this investigation of linguistic/mathematical interaction. Paul agreed that he was taller but thinner than Mark. Mark, however, having stated he was wider than Paul, could not (or would not) continue to the 'but' stage.

Comparisons extended to more than two

Number (ordering)

Seriation, or putting in order, is an activity relevant to the two aspects of number: cardinal (expressing how many) and ordinal (relating to order). In the early stages, children's learning of these concepts generally develops separately, then they come to appreciate that when they have, say, counted to the third object in a row, that object together with the two preceding it form a set with the cardinal number 3. Such is the presupposition behind counting, and indeed the number line.

Fig. 3.9 is a graph requiring the use of both concepts. Note the method, which the children have doubtless acquired from their teacher, of preparing a framework so that when names are written in they align horizontally. This produces a clear picture of the order of preference and the differences in the number of votes for each choice. You can read how *Mark and Me* used the representation to draw their conclusions. Obviously, *Me* found it tiring!

Size (Extension of number of attributes)

The first example is straightforward, and a most popular activity with children as it concerns their oft-repeated claim, "Mine is the biggest." It can therefore often be introduced naturally in response to such a claim rather than contrived. Take the following example prompted by a child claiming to have the biggest library book to take home. Table 3.2 is a copy of five children's comparisons and ordering of their books. (Letters A to E were stuck on the books with adhesive removeable labels.)

The children then described how their own books

Fig. 3.9 (above)

Table 3.2 (right)

→ is longer than	B	→	D	→	A	→	E	→	C
	(1st)		(2nd)		(3rd)		(4th)		(5th)
→ is wider than	D	→	A	→	B	→	C	→	E
	(1st)		(2nd)		(3rd)		(4th)		(5th)
→ is thicker than	B	→	E	→	A	→	C	→	D
	(1st)		(2nd)		(3rd)		(4th)		(5th)
→ weighs more than	B	→	A	→	D	→	C	→	E
	(1st)		(2nd)		(3rd)		(4th)		(5th)

Fig. 3.10

compared with the others. The owner of B, the vociferous claimant of having the biggest, reluctantly qualified this to his having the longest, thickest and heaviest one, and the one "wider than C and E". (For ordering as a lead into measurement, see page 37.)

A second similar example that caused a problem arose when a class of younger girls compared the sizes of their bears. All went well with groups that had the standard type, but in one an oddity appeared, namely Jumbo (see Fig. 3.10). Fig. 3.10 is the group leader's sketch which illustrates the height ordering:

Jumbo → Teddy → Mark → Paddington → Annabel.

The problem was that, although Jumbo was the 'biggest', he was hand-made and stuffed with feathers, so proved light to handle. The smaller bears were compact in comparison and therefore heavier. When an ordering was sought using a balance, this caused consternation because the sizes gave no clue to the masses (weights). (The use of 'mass' rather than 'weight', for example kilogram 'mass' rather than 'weight', is creeping gradually into general usage. This causes a confusion probably best expressed by a lad (aged 7 years) who stated in sheer perplexity, "To weigh with weights makes sense. Do we now mass with masses?")

Mass and volume are two quite different properties possessed by objects, and an ordering on the basis of mass is much more difficult to do than an ordering by, say, length. The problem that arose with the bears was to do with the density of the substances used for the stuffing (that is, mass per unit, say grams per cubic centimetre, of feathers compared with customary stuffing) and was not wholly to do with the perceptual impression of size (volume) as the girls had thought.

Similar problems can arise quite fortuitously in the classroom and in everyday living. Here are two further examples: one arose in a test and the other naturally.

A group of eight-year old pupils were shown four identical jars: one containing sand, one soap flakes, one water, and one peas, all reaching identical levels. The pupils were then asked, "In what order, heaviest to lightest, would you place these jars?" The unanimous verdict of the group was, "Peas first because they are bigger, sand next because it is darker, flakes next because they are lighter, and water last because we can see through it."

The second example involves another group of eight-year olds who were to bring pets to school to weigh the next day. They found there was only one commercially produced kilogram mass in school so, to be on the safe side, they decided to make more in plasticine. They took it in turns to place the kilogram mass on one side of the scale, and then balanced it with the right amount of plasticine to make the same mass. All happily tidied up their 'lumps', except one boy (Roy) who spent every spare moment moulding and beating his. When asked why, he explained, "to get it the same size as the real one – it's wrong". On hearing of this, the secondary physics teacher was so intrigued he came to talk to Roy (he gave as his opinion that understanding of mass generally develops at secondary age). Roy remained baffled. "Someday", said the teacher to the discouraged Roy, "I hope you will be in my class. We need thinkers like you." The boost was short-lived. As soon as he had left, John, one of the group who had edged in and listened, declaimed dismissively, "Don't be so dumb Roy – think about candy floss and as much toffee." Roy did. He then knew. (This reminds one of the time-honoured riddle 'Which weighs most: a ton of coal or a ton of feathers?'.)

In teaching, it is advisable to check that the influence of density does not intrude in comparisons (as it did with the bears), until pupils are ready to understand the concept. Jumbo *had* to be included on this occasion as the other owners had jeered at him. Children can be cruel!

Fig. 4.1 (left) Fig. 4.2 (above)
Fig. 4.3 (below) Fig. 4.4 (right)

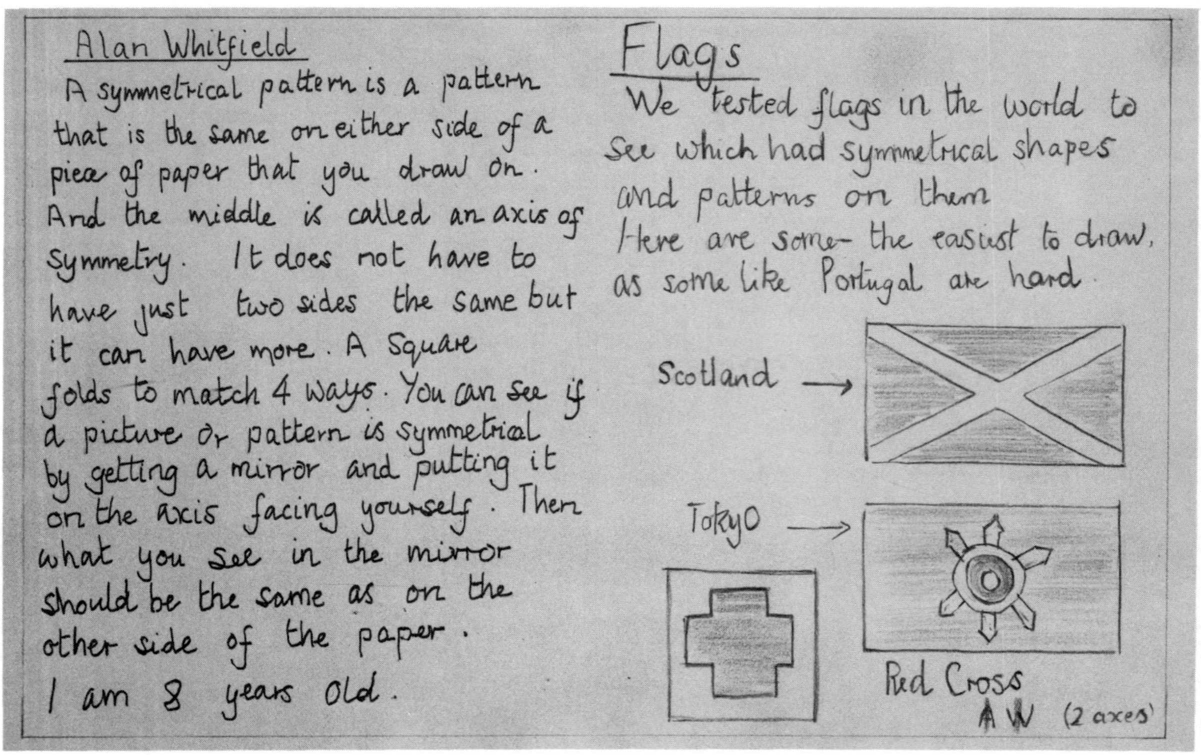

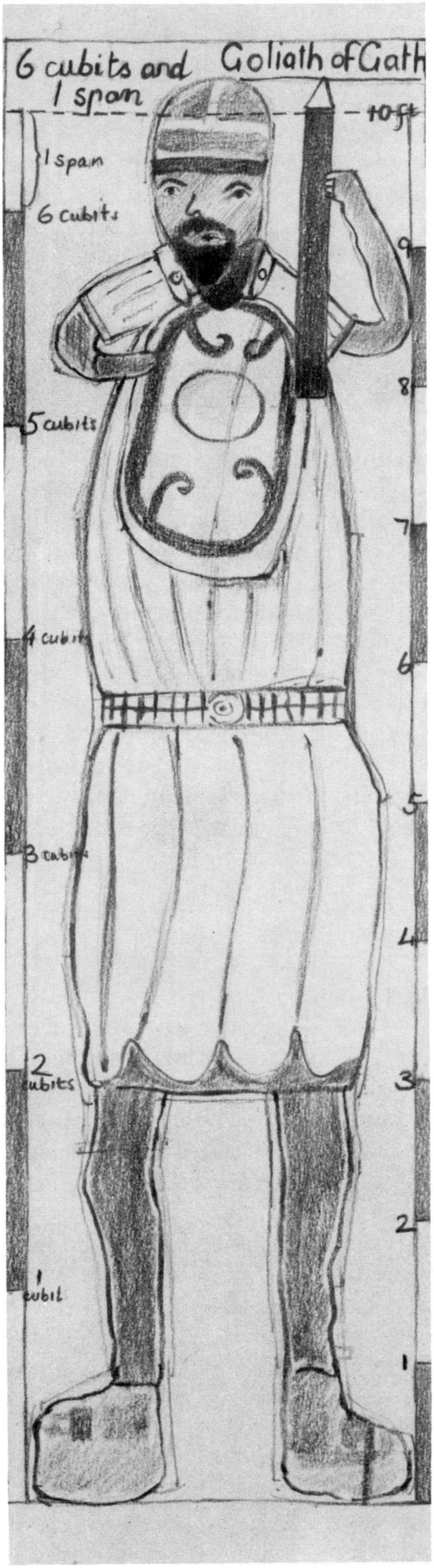

4 Shape and measurement

Symmetry

In general usage, symmetry often suggests proportionate presentation, balance, a kind of harmony. The more precise definition, however, of *bilateral symmetry* is the exact match of left and right as investigated in the introductory activities shown in Figs. 4.1–4.4 on page 34.

(Understanding of this aspect of symmetry is basic to the establishment of the commutative law in the next chapter, as are other aspects (rotational and reflection) to research into properties of regular polygons in Chapter 7.)

Measurement

This section provides a follow-up to the non-numerical comparisons of size and quantity experienced in the previous chapter. Here continuous quantities are measured in units. Unfortunately, confusion can exist between what is to be measured and the unit chosen to measure it. Ask, for example, "What is length?" and the reply, even from adults, may well be (pre-metric) "Length is feet" or, for capacity, "Capacity is pints." Early experience using a variety of units such as strides or spans for length, and cups, etc. for capacity can help to off-set such confusion with children and give a true impression of the concept of measurement.

Units

Let us consider an example of the flexibility younger children can exercise in choice of units if they understand their function. It occurred when a group of boys (aged 7–8 years) decided to draw a full-length sketch of David and Goliath (all six cubits and one span of him). Their own cubits (forearms) only produced a mini-giant, so they sought their Head Teacher to use his cubit and his span. They agreed that David's height should be about 5 feet.

To construct Goliath they:

(1) marked out his height in cubits and spans;
(2) marked it again, this time in feet so that his height was

really appreciated (They refused to use metres as they said "that would be like putting him in an aeroplane and he lived in Bible time – anyway in feet sounds bigger". Compare an opinion offered by John Cooper, Church's Correspondent, in an appraisal of the metric revision of the New English Bible. Of the Goliath incident he wrote, 'he was an enormous six cubits and a span in height. Making him "nearly 3 metres tall" really cuts him down to size and detracts from David's glory.');

(3) sketched him in, then painted a truly awesome figure.

In the meantime a most heroic portrait of David was completed.

It was then decided to fix them side by side on the classroom wall. Goliath was too tall for the wall, so he was fixed with his legs stretched out before him: an ignominous posture.

An American mathematician present at that time suggested, "Why not halve Goliath?" Noting their shock he added, "and David too, of course". "And make David wrong too", said the leader, "no". So chairs were fetched, put over his legs and a notice appended, 'STEP OVER MY LEGS'. The children did, and so did the mathematician.

Before offering a follow-up to the non-numerical comparisons given in the previous chapter, let us consider what is involved in measurement. This activity involves the measuring of a continuous quantity in units: the basis for comparison is the number of such units. It therefore has a quantitative and numerical aspect.

Introducing number

The change to metric units has highlighted the need for fractional parts since the larger units now in common use have replaced the smaller imperial units: for example the kilogram in place of the pound, the litre in place of the pint, and the metre leaving no counterpart to the useful foot. This makes it even more important to understand fractional parts, at least $\frac{1}{4}$, $\frac{1}{2}$ and $\frac{3}{4}$, from an early age and later to facilitate estimations and approximations.

I now offer two approaches to fractions, the second resulting from the reaction to the first.

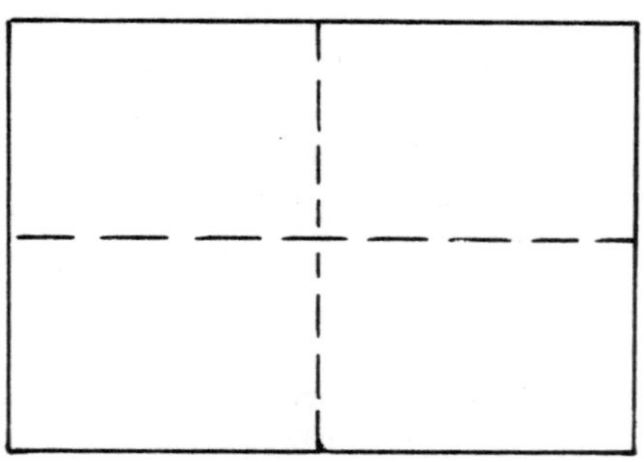

The first approach uses paper. A young boy folded and cut his rectangle of paper in half, and then in half again as requested by the teacher. When I asked what he was doing he replied, "Do you mean what teacher thinks I'm doing? She thinks I'll stick them down to make them all one again – but you can't ever never make them a whole again. Never." (*John aged 6 years*)

The second approach, using water, was chosen because it allows reversability. The apparatus consists of seven identical

Activity

1. Establish one whole (L and B).
2. Halve (L and B). Return to 1 – record halves.
3. Halve halves (L and B). Return $\frac{1}{4}$s to $\frac{1}{2}$s, then to 1 whole.

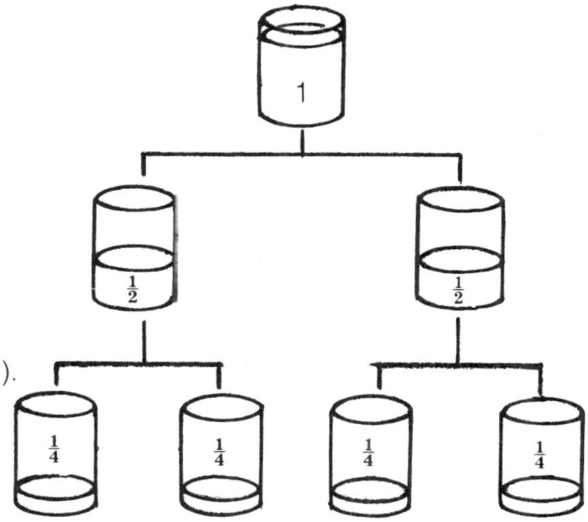

Recording

1

$\frac{1}{2} + \frac{1}{2} = \frac{2}{2} = 1$

$\frac{1}{4} + \frac{1}{4} = \frac{1}{2}$

$\frac{1}{4} + \frac{1}{4} + \frac{1}{4} + \frac{1}{4} = \frac{4}{4} = 1$

$(\frac{1}{2}) + \frac{1}{4} + \frac{1}{4} = 1$

Fig. 4.5

jars, adhesive labels (abbreviated to L in Fig. 4.5 when used to label the fraction), and rubber bands (abbreviated to B when used to mark the height of the water). Ongoing discussion and participation helps to establish understanding. $\frac{3}{4}$ evolves when dealing with $\frac{1}{4}$ and $\frac{1}{2}$.

With older pupils the extension can be made to eighths; a similar procedure can lead from $\frac{1}{2}$ to tenths. It can prove practical to write denominators first so that the share is established first, then the number of such shares. This helps in 'reading' a fraction, for example $\frac{7}{8}$. (So realistic can the water activity prove that on one occasion, when a few drops were spilt at the third stage, the activity had to be started again with a new whole.)

Now let us look at the greater precision that is possible in comparisons when measurement can be used. This example illustrates an extension in this respect from the example of the books (page 30). Here measurement not only provides the tool for finding actual differences, but also provides practice in those activities so essential throughout life, namely *estimating* and *approximating* to the nearest practicable unit.

Five girls (aged 10 years) decided to find the differences between their heights and masses, then later turned to length of strides. Fig. 4.6 shows them striding. Their names, in alphabetical order, are Amanda (A), Carol (C), Laura (La), Lisa (L), and Sally (S). They estimated their heights and masses (estimated measurements: E.M.), then found their actual measurements (A.M.). Fig. 4.7 shows their results.

Results of length of strides are not entered here, but when asked which one would take the least strides for a set distance, they agreed that it would be Susan, who had the longest stride.

It was not as straightforward for a group of young boys. On this occasion the group, then the whole class, agreed that

Fig. 4.6 (right)

Fig. 4.7

Height:	E.M.	A.M.
A	135 cm	133 cm
C	140 cm	142 cm
L	145 cm	144 cm
La	142 cm	140 cm
S	150 cm	157 cm

Order: → is taller than

S → L → C → La → A
157 cm 144 cm 142 cm 140 cm 133 cm

(D) 13 cm 2 cm 2 cm 7 cm

Mass:	E.M.	A.M.
A	30 kg	$25\frac{1}{2}$ kg
C	28 kg	$32\frac{1}{2}$ kg
L	25 kg	28 kg
La	31 kg	$29\frac{1}{2}$ kg
S	42 kg	40 kg

Order: → is heavier than

S → C → La → L → A
40kg $32\frac{1}{2}$ kg $29\frac{1}{2}$ kg 28 kg $25\frac{1}{2}$ kg

7 kg 3 kg $1\frac{1}{2}$ kg $2\frac{1}{2}$ kg

the one with the longest stride would need most strides. As no appreciable difference arose between their length of strides, a male member of staff was invited in and covertly advised to do his best. He with his longer stride needed the least number! Deep thinking resulted, then gradually the realisation dawned that, the longer the stride, the smaller the number needed. *In this way, the difficult concept of inverse ratio was grasped – no mean achievement.*

Returning to the girls, what was surprising was their worry at having only four differences: surely there should be five? A suggestion that they looked at their open hands resulted in a somewhat shamefaced retreat.

Perimeter and area

An illustration was offered on page 11 of how Peter used the glib response to a definition of area, namely, $A = l \times b$. The following example illustrates how a teacher of younger children (aged 7–8 years) introduced the concepts of perimeter and area in a practical way synonymous with their meaning. A leaf provided the apparatus and a string was put round it to find the perimeter. To find the area, the leaf was traced round on squared paper and the number of unit squares counted (part squares were combined). Julie's leaf shown in Fig. 4.8 led to a perimeter estimate of 16 cm and an actual measurement of 20 cm. It had an area estimate of 11 cm^2 and an actual measurement of 14 cm^2 approximately (square centimetres proved easier to deal with than square inches.)

A further example of measuring irregular areas arose when pupils (aged 10 years) were told by their science teacher that air pressure at sea level is 15 lb per square inch. Interest arose over what that pressure could mean on a body. John, the most restless boy, was chosen as a model to lie

Fig. 4.8 (below)

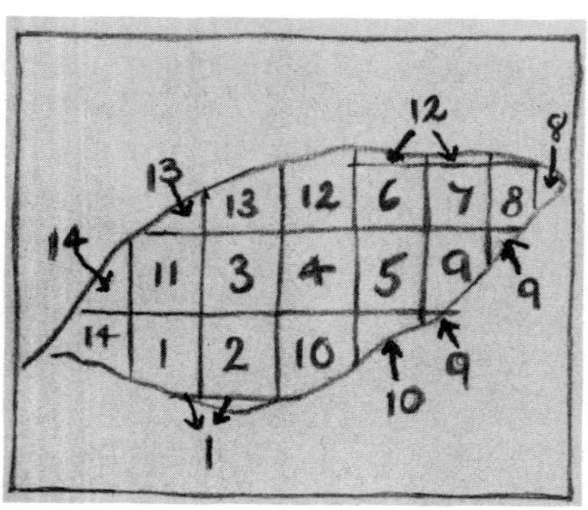

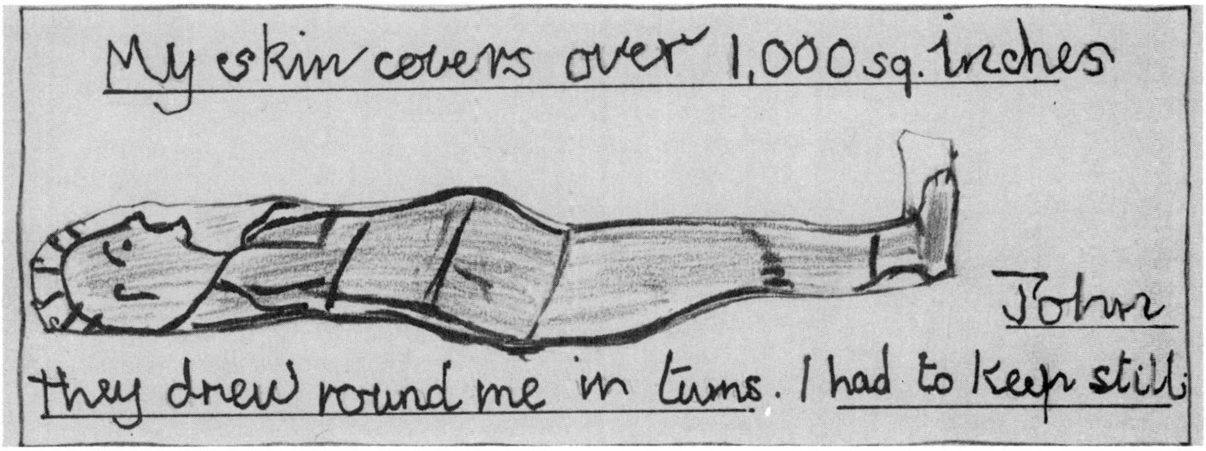

Fig. 4.9

motionless on paper marked in square inches, while he was drawn around first on his back and then on his side. The two results were doubled and added to find the approximate area of his whole body in square inches. Then, using calculators, the pupils reckoned the air pressure on John to be about 7 tons! John flew round telling everybody, till 'friends' deflated his exuberance by pointing out that he was not alone in his 'honour' (less politely expressed!). The question put to me, the visitor, was "Why doesn't it show when I stand on the scales?"

Central tendency

A teacher of ten-year-old pupils introduced them to all three methods of central tendency, namely median (middle), mode (most popular) and average (mean). Two simple activities provided a way for pupils to *understand* the latter (as opposed to knowing the rule, 'Add them all up and divide by the number there are'). The first one was to give out, say, 12 sweets per group in unequal shares, then pose the questions in turn, "How can they be shared equally between two pupils? Three pupils? Four pupils?" The second activity was to have two pupils (tall and small if possible) stretch out on the floor, provide string and scissors, and ask, "What height must each be to cover the same share of the total length?" Then use three pupils and four similarly. In short, find a fair share. The rule provides a computationally correct procedure.

This is how the class conducted their research using their own measurements. The account is by Joan, and is quoted here verbatim.

"This week we looked at ourselves. First we found our heights then we weighed ourselves. We wrote them both on a piece of paper and pinned ours on ourselves.

First we found the medians. It had stopped raining so we lined up outside, shortest to tallest. Then we cast off which left Wendy in the middle. She is *143 cm*. Then we lined up lightest to heaviest and cast off. John was left. He is *37 kg*.

Then we found the modes. To do it we stood together if we had the same measurements to see which was most popular. There were two answers, 140 and 143 cm, and 34 and 39 kg. Another class our age helped us out, and then it was 142 cm, and 36 kg.

Last we found the averages. We used our calculators to add them all up and divide by 29. The answers were 140 cm, and $37\frac{1}{2}$ kg."

Their results are shown in the table to the left.

	Median	Mode	Average
Height	143 cm	142 cm	140 cm
Mass	37 kg	36 kg	$37\frac{1}{2}$ kg

To complete the study, the teacher decided to let the class explore the correlation between heights and masses. First the scatter-diagram shown in Fig. 4.10 (to scale) was drawn for the girls' results, then the boys entered theirs on the girls' graph (circled points). The teacher was amazed to see that there was little, if any, difference due to sex.

Further investigation, based on separate averages, led to the second table.

Age 11 yrs	Average height	Average mass
Boys	144 cm	36 kg
Girls	$144\frac{1}{2}$ cm	38 kg

As a follow-up, interested teachers produced the third table for their own heights and masses, which gave less surprising results.

Adults	Average height	Average mass
Men	179 cm	70 kg
Women	165 cm	60 kg

The school doctor, being told of the class's results, suggested that the class be allowed to ring her at the clinic. Furnished with their 'statistics', the class leader dialled. The doctor said their results were supported by the fact that their age group was *the* one where this near parity could occur. She then advised them to try measuring younger children. (They were about to move to secondary school so there was no time to do this.)

Fig. 4.10

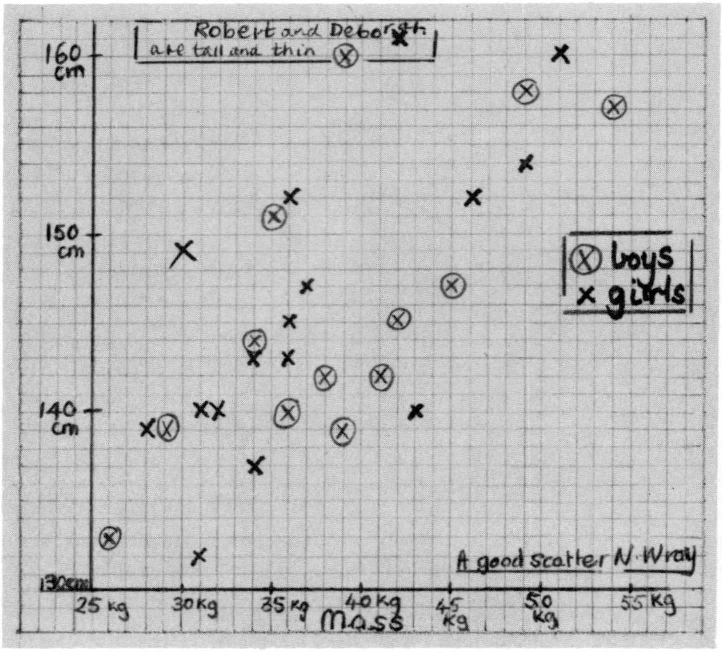

5 Arithmetical operations

It is unwise on social occasions to admit to an interest in mathematics. Invariably those on the fringe edge away, while those who are 'cornered' seek cover under remarks such as, "Oh maths (*restrained shudder*) – it was my worst subject", then add, almost defensively, "I was scared of it – I could never remember what to do." Their memory of that fear has persisted even into adulthood! What branch of mathematics mainly causes this reaction? Surely some degree of accountability lies with arithmetical operations.

Such a reaction suggests a background based on instrumental learning in which, to quote, 'processes are carried out properly to produce a "correct result"'. The weakness is self-evident: the 'proper' processes have to be memorised (as well as possibly the table facts which feed them). Unfortunately the weakness extends beyond that of the pupils, as it is skill in this memorising that is widely accepted as a criterion for successful learning in public/parental judgement. What then, by comparison, does an approach based on relational learning offer: primarily, of course, on educational grounds and then, as a subsidiary, in the field of public relations?

I now make the following claim, which I hope to substantiate through examples of reactions of pupils, namely, that relationships between operations, a timely use of laws and overall respect for the principle of order can:

(1) promote, through transfer of experience, less dependence on memorisation;
(2) help to establish facts (addition and multiplication) and almost halve the number of facts to be learnt;
(3) incorporate the learning of skills within a problem-solving reasoning approach and thereby provide opportunities for logical thinking rather than excluding it, that is extend the reasoning approach used in other areas rather than just 'doing sums'.

This chapter is in three parts. The first two describe the stages of development in achieving informed numeracy: (1) the *relationships between operations*; and (2) the *laws affecting operations* and the benefit derived from their combined application. Finally the *conclusion* gives opinions of informed numeracy by industry and in an H.M.I. report.

Experience with younger children made me very aware that progression in arithmetic could not be dismissed as working up from multiplication tables 2 to 10. In the early stages children need to make a very testing move, namely from merely comparing numbers as in Chapter 3 to dealing with a trio of them. This trio consists of first the number to be operated on, next the one involved in the operation and lastly the one giving the result. For example, 4+2=6 has trio (4,2,6), 4−2=2 (4,2,2), 4×2=8 (4,2,8), and 4÷2=2 (4,2,2). Also, multiplication tables require facts to be ordered. I would liken the complexity of learning this on a child level to that of an adult (or at least myself) learning to drive. The tutor needs a great deal of skill!

Relationships between operations

The 'tree' in Fig. 5.1, illustrating the stemming of arithmetical operations from addition in the first instance, is of practical value to have in mind when introducing a new operation to young children, or meeting an obvious difficulty with older ones. (The emergence of addition as a mental abstract operation is illustrated on page 19.)

Note: The four suits in a set of playing cards are used as examples here.

Fig. 5.1

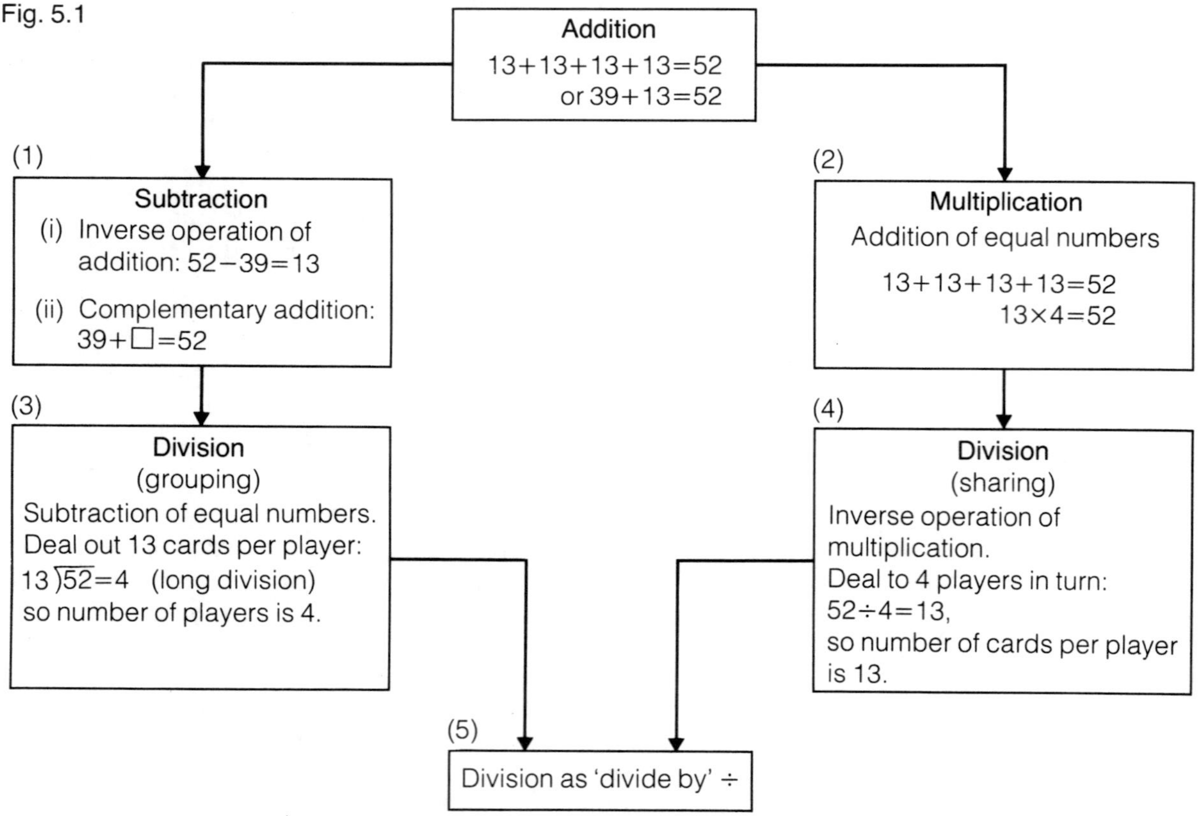

The transitions numbered (1) to (5) in Fig. 5.1 will now be discussed in that order. Inverse relations (+, −), (×, ÷) follow.

Subtraction as complementary addition

This method can prove most effective in promoting quick mental calculations. Compare the examples here with the usual inverse addition method.

24	101	1000
−19	− 93	− 989
as 19+ [5] =24	as 93+ [8] =101	as 989+ [11] =1000

Shopping activities lead naturally into this common form of subtraction. For example, start with a 50p coin and a purchase costing 33p. Then, to work out how much change we shall get, we ask what we need to add to 33p to make 50p: answer 17p.

In this context, I had a most salutary experience. One morning, Dawn, who had a reputation for not understanding 'difference' (see page 12), and I met in a supermarket. Her basket was almost full and Dawn, with her usual broad beam, said, "I've almost finished 'cause I've spent up", then added, for my benefit, "See, I had £5 to start with and I've spent £4.60 – so I've only got up to £1 left – only 40p."

I did not even know what I had spent so had not a hope of predicting what I had left – even though I could define complementary addition!

Multiplication as addition of equal numbers

×	0	1	2	3	4	5	→	10
0	0	0	0	0	0	0	...	0
1	0	1	2	3	4	5	...	10
2	0	2	4	6	8	10	...	20
3	0	3	6	9	12	15	...	30
4	0	4	8	12	16	20	...	40
5	0	5	10	15	20	25	...	50
↓	⋮	⋮	⋮	⋮	⋮	⋮		⋮
10	0	10	20	30	40	50	...	100

In this method, table sequences are built up by repeated addition. Young children can use three-dimensional material to help them 'build' the tables, for example wheels (cycles for 2, tricycles for 3, cars for 4). Coloured blocks are also useful.

This is a practical way to learn table facts. Sequences can be said across fingers to help establish them. This method can also be used to correct hazy knowledge with older children (it replaces the by then childish table chanting, which I confess I loathe).

Further, when tens and units are introduced, the comparison, as in the example here, makes sense of long multiplication, which might otherwise be learned as a meaningless rule.

17→	17
+17	× 5
+17	85
+17	
+17	
85	

Note that the same procedure takes place in both: it is then clear why the 3 (30) from 35 is added to the tens column.

Division as subtraction of equal numbers (*grouping*)

This concept of division involves considering 8 ÷ 2 (say) as 'how many 2s are there in 8?'. It leads into what for many has been regarded as the *bête noire* of operations, namely long division. A headmistress described how she was taught it. "One Monday morning (to be fresh for the ordeal) the teacher strode in, wrote the following sentence on the board and decoded it as shown."

---

don't	try	putting	muddy	socks	back	on
↓	↓	↓	↓	↓	↓	↓
(d)	(t)	(p)	(m)	(s)	(b)	(o)
↓	↓	↓	↓	↓	↓	↓
divide	try	put	multiply	subtract	bring down	on

This rule is applied as follows (mnemonic letters included):

$$\begin{array}{r} 2 \\ 31\overline{)669} \\ 62 \\ \hline 49 \end{array}$$

(d) 3s into 6 = 2: (t) 2 × 31 = 62: (p) 2 in the answer (where?)

(m) 2 × 31 = 62

(s) 2 from 6 is 4: (b) bring down 9

(o) on, (repeat from d)

"Mind you", she added, "I could always divide if I remembered 'my socks'". (I suspect, however, that, with this method, problems have arisen through the habit of omitting the zero, i.e. writing 62 instead of 620.) I once, for interest, wrote this very example on the board [669 ÷ 31] and explained to the pupils (aged 8+ years) that we would be trying it the next day, so why not have a try that night themselves. One girl, admittedly advised by a parent who told her this was long division, used a sheet of foolscap and repeatedly subtracted 31. It was certainly a long effort, and as certainly right. The introduction to block grouping was there. A class effort followed, resulting in the subtraction of twenty 31s first as the winner.

$$\begin{array}{rl} 21 \text{ r. } 8 & \\ 31\overline{)669} & \\ -620 & \rightarrow 31 \times 20 \\ \hline 49 & \\ -\ 31 & \rightarrow 31 \times 1 \\ \hline 8 & \end{array}$$

Division as the inverse operation of multiplication (sharing)

In this concept of division, 8 ÷ 2 is considered as 'what is 8 shared between 2?' A period exists between children being able to deal with this aspect in a concrete situation and calculating. They can share, for example, 12 objects between say 4 of them (3 × 4 = 12, $\frac{1}{4}$ of 12 = 3) but to extend to $\frac{1}{12}$ of 84 would puzzle them even if they remember 7 × 12 = 84. Of interest, how would you find $\frac{1}{31}$ of 629?

Division meaning 'divide by' (÷)

Confusion often arises between the two aspects of division (grouping and sharing). In Fig. 5.2 they are illustrated in graphical form. Diagram (a) illustrates grouping in twos, for example number of 2s in 8 is 4. Diagram (b) illustrates sharing between two, for example 8 shared between 2 is 4. (Do we always note the distinction?)

Combine the ideas illustrated in (a) and (b):

(a) $2\overline{)8} = 4$ and (b) $\frac{1}{2}$ of $8 = 4$.
The answer is the same:
8 divided by $2 = 4$,
$8 \div 2 = 4$.

Children need to go through three stages:

(1) using grouping and sharing as two different operations;
(2) relating them (as here);
(3) progressing to the use of 'divide by' (÷) as we do, knowing that the answer will be the same. (How did you find $\frac{1}{31}$ of 629?)

Fig. 5.2

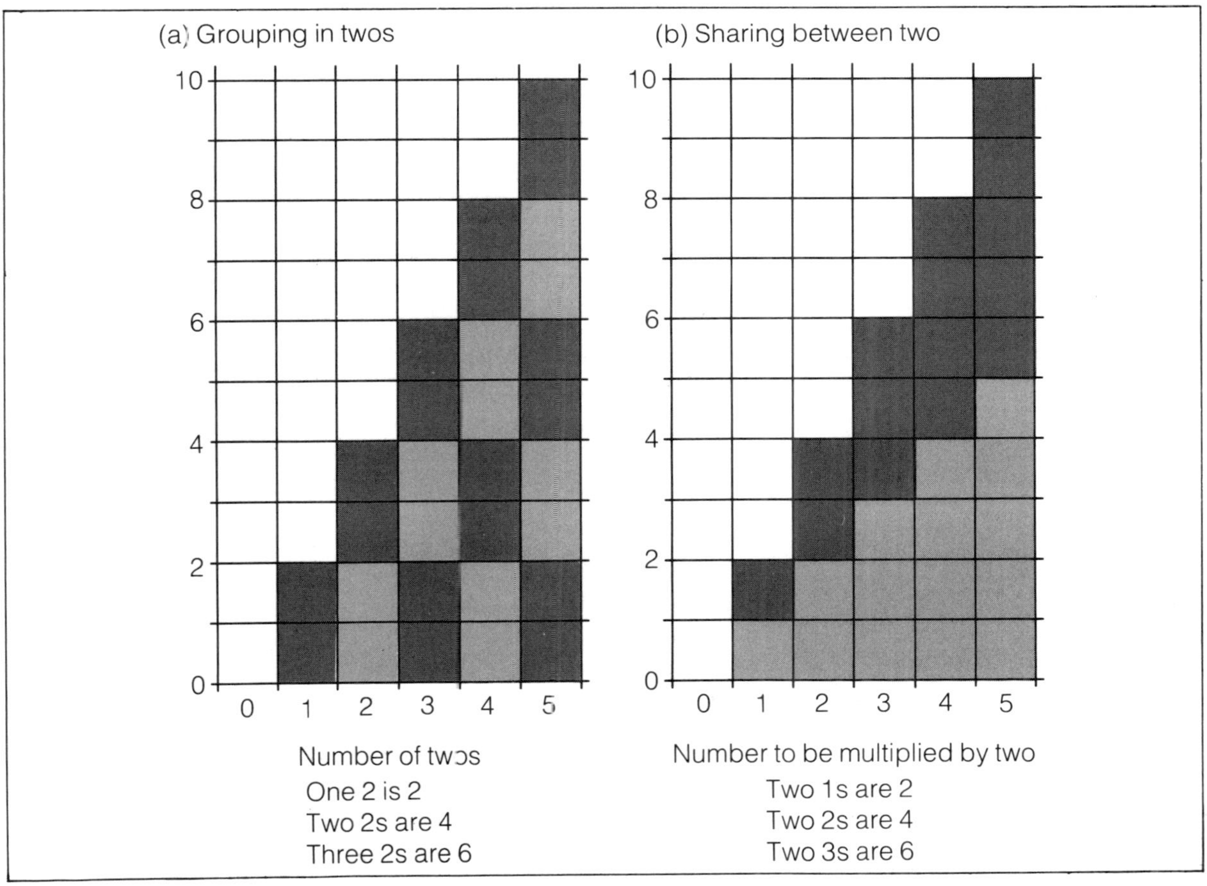

Inverse relations

Note: Structural apparatus, for example Unifix or coloured blocks, can be used to establish inverses. Examples are

(a) $5+3=8$ Join 5 red blocks and 3 blue blocks: total 8.
$8-3=5$ Take off 3 blue blocks: 5 left.

(b) $4\times3=12$ Join 4 sets of 3: total 12.
$12\div3=4$ Take off in sets of 3: 4 sets.

Fig. 5.3 is a diagrammatic representation for the four operations showing how they are inverses of each other.

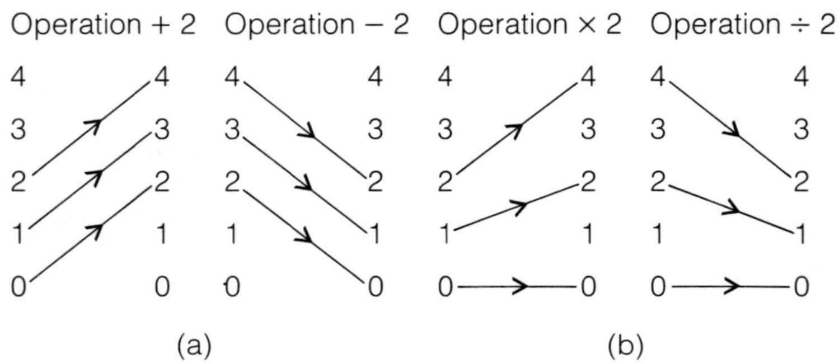

Laws affecting operations

The three laws to be discussed are unfortunately blessed with rather high-sounding names, especially considering their common practical use. They are as follows.

(1) *The commutative law*
(known to children as the changeover law)
This means in practice
$a+b = b+a$, for example $7+6 = 6+ 7$;
$a\times b = b\times a$, for example $7\times6 = 6\times 7$.

(2) *The distributive law*
This is basically a description of the common practice used when multiplying by numbers greater than 10, for example calculating 17×13 as
$17(10+3) = (17\times10)+(17\times3)$,
i.e. 13 is distributed as $10+3$.

(3) *The associative law*
This law means that we can add or multiply numbers in any order. It says that $(a+b)+c=a+(b+c)$, so brackets are unnecessary: $a+b+c$ or $2+3+4$ may be added in any order.

Similarly, $a \times b \times c$ or $2 \times 3 \times 4$ may be multiplied in any order.

Let me give a warning about (1) and (3). We are so aware as adults that the order of numbers can be changed over to suit our needs in addition and multiplication that we may take it as a known fact for children (I have checked with secondary pupils and have found their awareness of this is only hazy). This uncertainty can be a great handicap for, as will be proved later, knowledge about (1) can halve the number of facts (+ and ×) that need to be known.

The commutative law

The first stage involves assembling facts with the same sum or product and ordering them. Here is an *introduction (for addition)* via Harold (aged 8 years), as it appeared in *Press Report* (San Diego).

Dora Whittaker of Nottingham, England won't forget Harold for some time to come. He is one of 27 students in a second grade class who recently participated in a math 'demonstration'. In the same room was an audience of teachers and administrators.

The 'manipulatives' were five of the children. Using hoops she had, at their suggestion, three boys stand in one hoop and two girls in the other. Then the arrangements were changed for reasons offered by them to one and four, then five and zero – arrangements recorded in turn on the blackboard as in A, then ordered as in B.

A		B
3+2=5	(boys/girls)	0+5=5
2+3=5	(girls/boys)	1+4=5
1+4=5	(9yrs/8yrs)	2+3=5
4+1=5	(8yrs/9yrs)	3+2=5
5+0=5	(children/adults)	4+1=5
0+5=5	(adults/children)	5+0=5

Harold's attention remained fixed on the blackboard. Then, all at once he made the sudden discovery. "Hey Keith", he bellowed out, oblivious of anyone or anything but his friend and the blackboard, "I don't know which one of these pairs got backwards but I do know that 1+4 backwards is 4+1. Who said that 1+4 is to come first 'cause it really doesn't matter – they both make 5. Can you see that Keith?". Keith couldn't. Harold understood now that all pairs of numbers could be reversed and all add up to the same sum. He was ecstatic over his discovery.

And so was I. Where I could have failed, Harold ceeded (except for convincing Keith).

In the context of *addition* it was an introduction to n bers and their ordering that I had in mind when I advisedly sent 'back to base' by Harold. An example of m propitious timing occurred in Florida when I had taken week's course with teachers of remedial mathematics, ar was then invited to teach one of their classes. In respect fo the comparative maturity of the students (aged 14–15 years) I used rods for manipulatives, and mapping as a form recording (new to them). They worked in pairs selecting t own sum. Fig. 5.4 is a copy of one pair's work on Harol as the constant sum.

And now to *multiplication*. The commutative law can be approached visually by looking, for example, at a carton of half a dozen eggs. One view gives $2 \times 3 = 6$, and another gives $3 \times 2 = 6$. Facts about 6 as a constant product can be set out as shown in Fig. 5.5.

The position of the relationships shown in Figs. 5.4 and 5.5 will be circled on the charts which follow (Figs. 5.6 and 5.7).

Note: These mappings illustrate what is recorded algebraically as follows:

Fig. 5.4 shows the constant sum $x + y = c$ (here $c = 5$)
Fig. 5.5 shows the constant product $xy = c$ (here $c = 6$)
(For the graph of $xy = c$ where $c = 8$, see page 56.)

A confirmation of the law (for addition and multiplication) can be effected through investigation of the symmetrical properties of the charts in Figs. 5.6 and 5.7.

Fig. 5.4

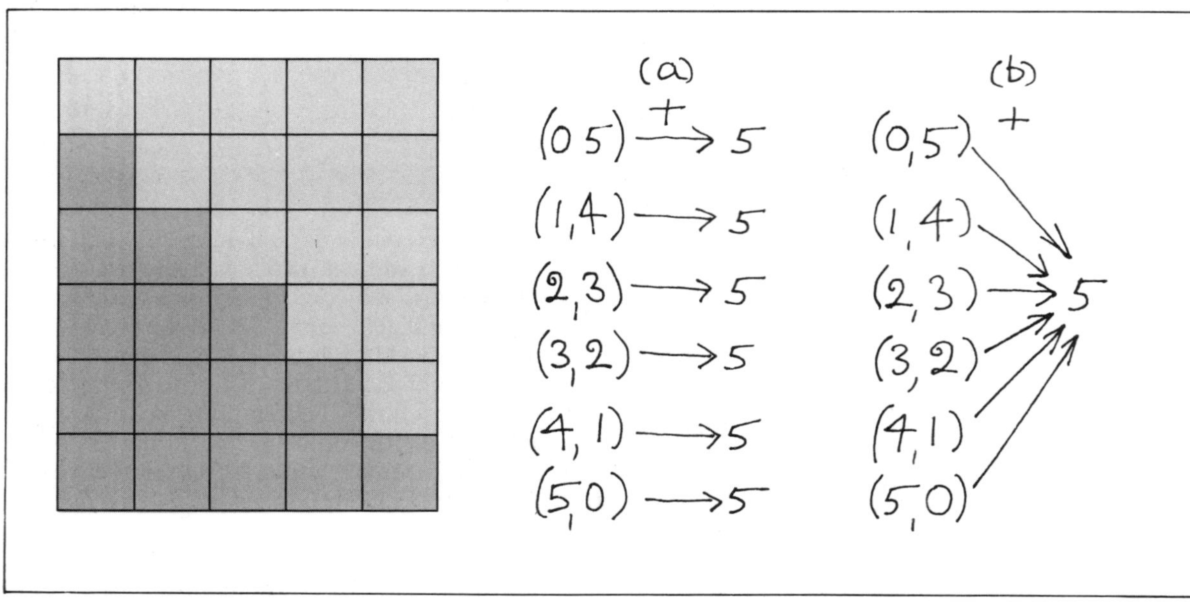

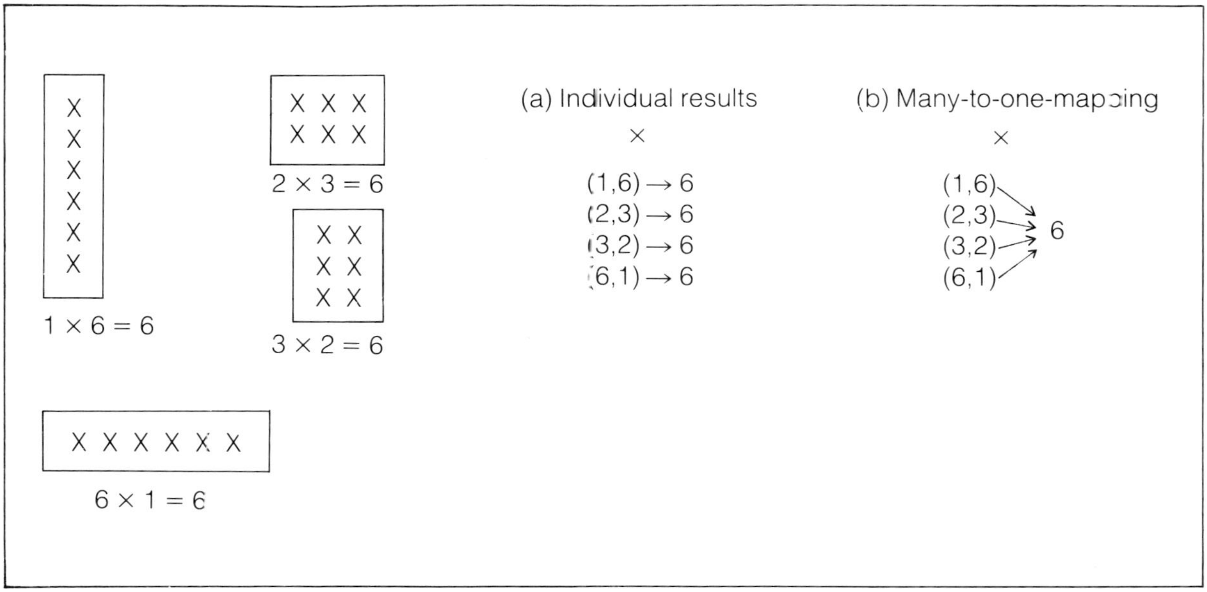

+	0	1	2	3	4	5	6	7	8	9	10
0	0	1	2	3	4	5	6	7	8	9	10
1	1	2	3	4	5	6	7	8	9	10	11
2	2	3	4	5	6	7	8	9	10	11	12
3	3	4	5	6	7	8	9	10	11	12	13
4	4	5	6	7	8	9	10	11	12	13	14
5	5	6	7	8	9	10	11	12	13	14	15
6	6	7	8	9	10	11	12	13	14	15	16
7	7	8	9	10	11	12	13	14	15	16	17
8	8	9	10	11	12	13	14	15	16	17	18
9	9	10	11	12	13	14	15	16	17	18	19
10	10	11	12	13	14	15	16	17	18	19	20

axis

×	0	1	2	3	4	5	6	7	8	9	10
0	0	0	0	0	0	0	0	0	0	0	0
1	0	1	2	3	4	5	6	7	8	9	10
2	0	2	4	6	8	10	12	14	16	18	20
3	0	3	6	9	12	15	18	21	24	27	30
4	0	4	8	12	16	20	24	28	32	36	40
5	0	5	10	15	20	25	30	35	40	45	50
6	0	6	12	18	24	30	36	42	48	54	60
7	0	7	14	21	28	35	42	49	56	63	70
8	0	8	16	24	32	40	48	56	64	72	80
9	0	9	18	27	36	45	54	63	72	81	90
10	0	10	20	30	40	50	60	70	80	90	100

axis

Fig. 5.5 (top)

Fig. 5.6 (above left) Addition chart

Fig. 5.7 (above right) Multiplication chart

The diagonals from left to right provide axes of symmetry. Pupils can find them by construcing their own charts, then folding on the diagonal in such a way that a number on the top fold matches (pricks through with a pin to) the same number on the lower fold. This demonstrates commutativity. For example,

in Fig. 5.6, 13 as 6 + 7 pierces 13 as 7 + 6 giving
$6 + 7 = 7 + 6$;
in Fig. 5.7, 42 as 6 × 7 pierces 42 as 7 × 6 giving
$6 \times 7 = 7 \times 6$.

The claim made earlier has been substantiated, namely that only half the number of table facts need to be learnt. For table sufferers this is as if some ghastly medicine had been reduced to half dosage.

It is interesting to observe the reaction from children aged 10–11 years. Teachers of this age group have found this a most effective way to ensure awareness of the commutative law and, further, it was taken up with zest. Children enjoyed the activity! Working in groups, one such class found that the *lines* on either side of the axes were repeats. For example, in Fig. 5.6 the line just above the axis 1, 3, 5, ..., 19 repeats the one just below the axis. In Fig. 5.7 the line just above the axis 0, 2, 6, ..., 90 also repeats the one just below, and so on. "This", the children said, "explains why the two *sides* repeat". Teachers also found that the children became intrigued with numbers and the patterns in the numbers. "Almost unbelievable", said one of them. I met the same reaction with secondary pupils.

The examples investigated earlier with constant sum 5 and constant product 6 are ringed on the charts. They and similar constant sums and products are endemic to the symmetry of the charts.

An original way to fill in the multiplication chart was discovered by Paul Zawadjiki (aged $9\frac{1}{2}$ years). Paul was a reticent boy who was fascinated by numbers. This was one of his self-motivated investigations. He had studied the multiplication chart with his group. Here is his description.

"I noticed the row that goes 5, 8, 9, 8, 5. I had seen it before. When? Yes, it was at the school before this when we did rectangles that have the same perimeters. So I drew some with perimeters of 12. Then I drew some more with perimeters of 14 and 16. I have put circles round 5, 8, 9, 8, 5 on my chart for perimeter 12.

Fig. 5.8

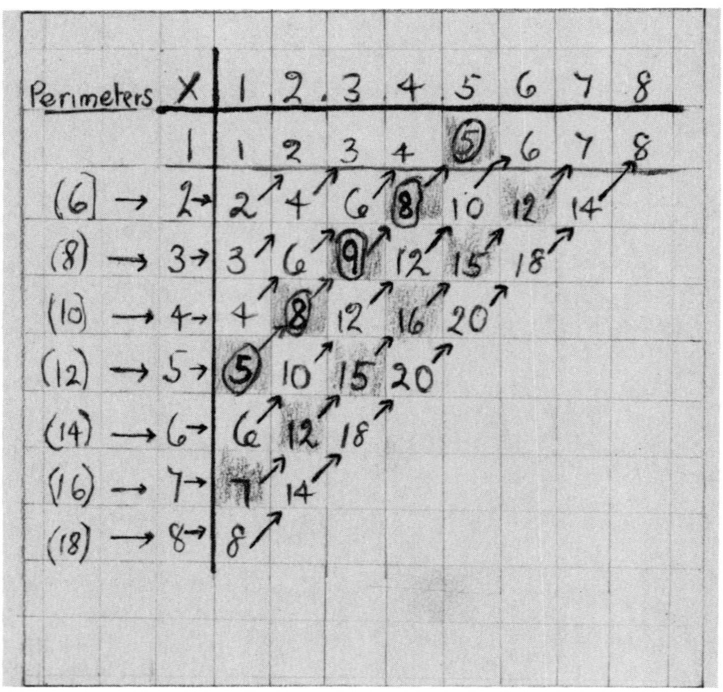

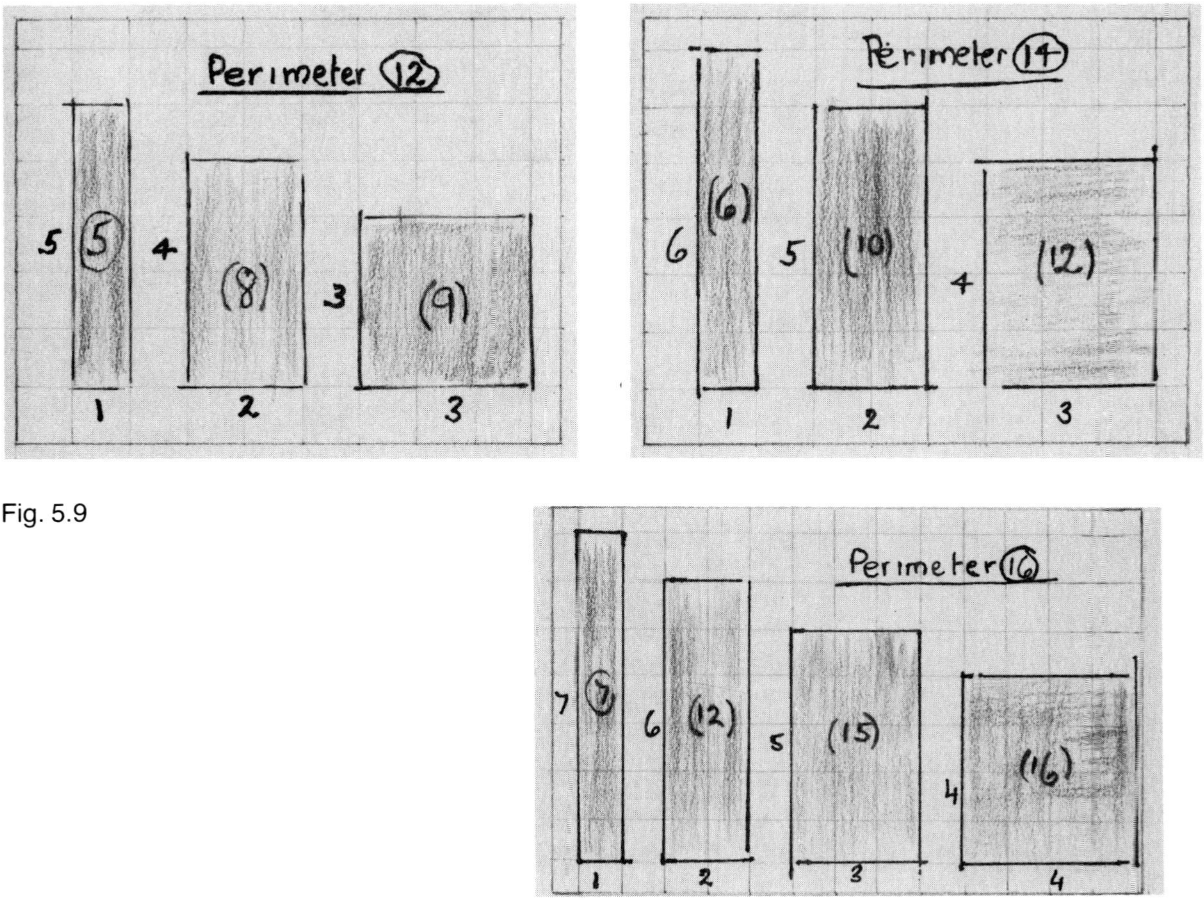

Fig. 5.9

You just turn them on their sides to finish the rows, so the rows are

perimeter (12) 5, 8, 9, 8, 5
perimeter (14) 6, 10, 12, 12, 10, 6
perimeter (16) 7, 12, 15, 16, 15, 12, 7
perimeter (18) 8, 14, 18, 20, 20, 18, 14, 8
– I did the last one by pattern.

I put the perimeters on my chart like you can see across from their own lines. It was easy to go back by pattern and do the first rows – perimeter (10) is 4, 6, 6, 4, perimeter (8) is 3, 4, 3 and perimeter (6) is 2, 2.

At first I could not think why. I thought about it for a week. Then I put the measurements for width and height on my rectangles. These are the same numbers you multiply for the chart.

See $1 \times 5 = 5$, $2 \times 4 = 8$, $3 \times 3 = 9$, $4 \times 2 = 8$, and $5 \times 1 = 5$.

The others work the same. It makes sense, but I'm still thinking about it."

(Compare the graph made by secondary pupils for width/area of rectangles: Fig. 3.3.)

Row	×	0	1	2	3	4	5	6 ···10
	0	0	0	0	0	0	0	0
a	1	0	1	2	3	4	5	6
b	2	0	2	4	6	8	10	12
c	3	0	3	6	9	12	15	18
d	4	0	4	8	12	16	20	24
e	5	0	5	10	15	20	25	30
	⋮ 10							

Fig. 5.10

The distributive law

This is just a ponderous title for a commonplace mathematical activity which takes place in multiplication by numbers over 10. For example 17 × 13 may be calculated as (17×10) + (17×3) with 13 distributed as 10 + 3 (13 being the multiplier). Is there only one choice, or are other options open? The answer comes from use of the distributive law.

Pupils can establish the law by a study of this section of the multiplication chart (Fig. 5.10). The options with 5 as multiplier are to add row a (numbers × 1) to row d (numbers × 4) or to add row b (numbers × 2) to row c (numbers × 3). For example, 6 × 5 = (6 × 1) + (6 × 4) or (6 × 2) + (6 × 3)

I watched a group of able juniors find the options available for multiplication by 2, 3, ..., 10. A pattern evolved.

Let us return to 17 × 13. One suspects that the customary practice of using the pairing (17×3) + (17×10) is adopted because it provides the simplest method for calculation, especially if there is in mind the nonsensical rule 'to multiply by 10 add 0'. Pupils can often be worried, even so. Should they find (17×3) then (17×10), or the reverse, thinking order matters? This reveals a lack of understanding, which can be clarified if other pairings are also used.

The associative law

This law used with the commutative law allows numbers to be associated in any order. In practice this facilitates quick calculations. Indeed, before the era of calculators, those dealing with accounts were often experts in its application. First let us look at an example in addition: 57 + 24 + 43 + 52 + 76. The units may be added as (7 + 3) + (6 + 4) + 2, i.e. 10 + 10 + 2. The tens may be combined similarly as (5 + 5) + (4 + 7) + 2, i.e. 10 + 11 + 2. Or, in one operation, (57 + 43) + (24 + 76) + 52. i.e. 100 + 100 + 52. I knew a boy (aged 11 years) who could 'beat' a calculator this way.

$$\begin{array}{r} 57 \\ +\,24 \\ +\,43 \\ +\,52 \\ +\,76 \\ \hline \end{array}$$

A rearrangement can also save effort in multiplication. For example write 25 × 19 × 2 as 19 × (25 × 2) = 19 × 50 = 950.

Lastly, here is a method of making a quick calculation which evolved when Miss S arranged a competition to find as many ways as possible of working out 67 × 8. Options employed ranged from addition only, multiplication by doubling and redoubling or trebling, or a mixture of both operations, to use of the distributive law and then to one inaugurated by the winner (as she had to be). She used subtraction as follows. Write 67 × 8 as [(67 × 9) − (67 × 1)], [(67 × 10) − (67 × 2)], [(67 × 11) − (67 × 3)], ... The class accepted defeat. Who can fight the infinite? This method is particularly good with, for example, the calculation of five articles at £1.99 each as (£2 × 5) − 5p or 67 × 99 as (67 × 100) − 67.

These suggestions are not as intensive in application as their coverage in one chapter might suggest. The span in time might well be from early primary (age 6 years) to pre-secondary (age 11 years): each progression being introduced as deemed advisable.

Teachers' research with older children produced the same objective which prompted me to move to teach younger children, namely to discover where lapses could have occurred in earlier experience, and the methods which could be used both to discover and deal with them. The added bonus that pupils became 'intrigued with numbers' in the process I find most rewarding: proof of the value of a reasoning approach compared with an instrumental one (as was claimed in the Introduction).

Conclusion

Before leaving this analysis for your appraisal, I offer for consideration this opinion on informed numeracy. It is part of a recommendation offered in the aforementioned Cockcroft Report, namely that pupils need to develop high powers of mental arithmetic, and working "done in the head" should occupy a central place in mathematics. Strong support comes from industry. Industrial apprentices should, for example, be able to estimate their earnings at say £2.50 per hour without elaborate calculations. On the job, they should, if required, be able to work out a circumference (approximately) by assessing a diameter – or even 'whipping' a ruler across it – and trebling that measurement (not stand there trying to remember if the formula is πd or πr^2 or $2\pi r$ or what?). Further, if they do calculate, they should be able to check their answer and know that they have 'not come up with rubbish'.

I conclude this analysis of means for promoting a logical approach to the acquisition of skills with this quotation from an H.M.I. appraisal of British schools. The section is entitled *The Need for Understanding*: 'In time past there was a market value in being able to calculate, without necessarily being able to interpret the results. The value of this is diminishing all the time. The entrant to industry needs to know what he is doing as well as to be able to do it (have informed numeracy): equally, when mathematics is taught to young pupils for non-vocational reasons, understanding is every bit as important.' I would maintain that such understanding results from a problem-solving approach with progressions at all times taking the form of logical extensions from what is known to what can be deduced.

6 Graphical representation of relationships

Relationships in the multiplication chart

Related pairs of numbers in multiplication have been found already in the previous chapter when pupils explored relationships in the chart. The progression here is to plot related

×	0	1	2	3	4	5	6	7	8	9	10	Times table
0	0	0	0	0	0	0	0	0	0	0	0	
1	0	1	2	3	4	5	6	7	(8)	9	10	×1
2	0	2	4	6	(8)	10	12	14	16	18	20	×2
3	0	3	6	9	12	15	18	21	24	27	30	×3
4	0	4	(8)	12	16	20	24	28	32	36	40	×4
5	0	5	10	15	20	25	30	35	40	45	50	×5
6	0	6	12	18	24	30	36	42	48	54	60	×6
7	0	7	14	21	28	35	42	49	56	63	70	×7
8	0	(8)	16	24	32	40	48	56	64	72	80	×8
9	0	9	18	27	36	45	54	63	72	81	90	×9
10	0	10	20	30	40	50	60	70	80	90	100	×10

(Column headings: x values)

Fig. 6.1

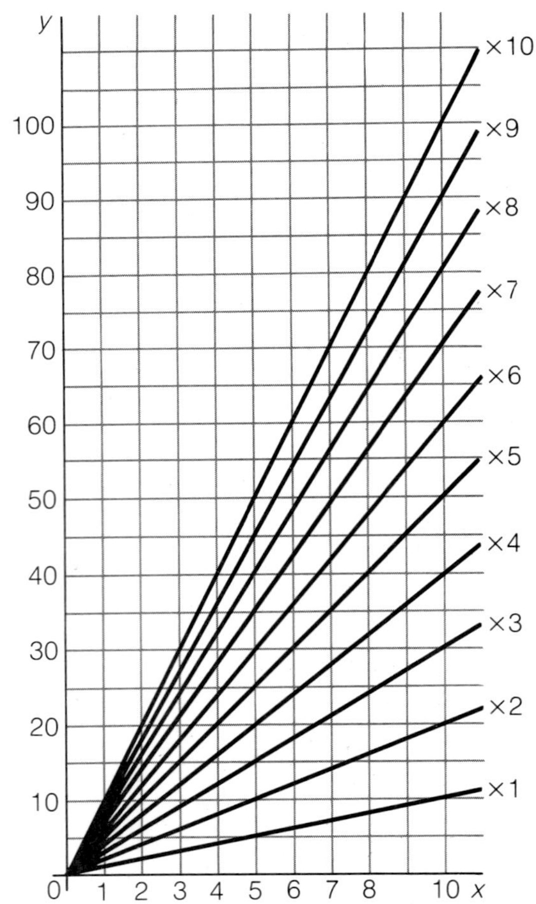

Fig. 6.2 (right) Graphs of the times tables

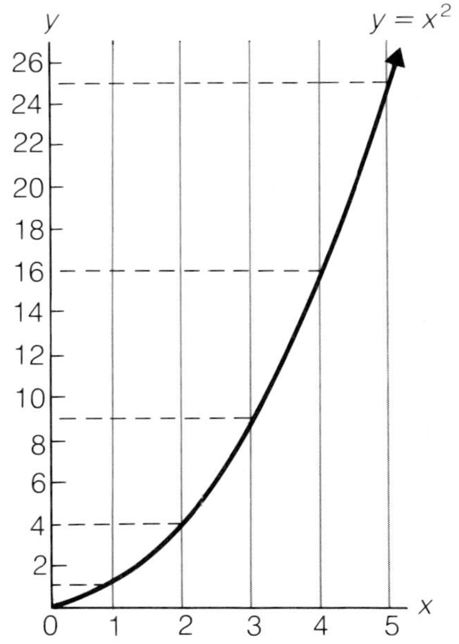

Fig. 6.3 (above)

Fig. 6.4 (below)

pairs on graphs as $x\,y$ relationships. Children enjoy this activity; as one child put it, "it sounds grown-up but it's easy".

One way that has proved practical is to have a copy of the multiplication chart, and to work from it (Fig. 6.1). Multiplicands are across the top of the chart, multipliers are down the left side, and products are inside the chart. Now we shall consider several examples of ordered pairs and the graphs obtained from them. Plotted pairs (x, y) are multiplicands (x) and products (y).

Example: times table 10 $(y = 10x)$
(0, 0), (1, 10), (2, 20), ..., (10, 100).
The graphs for times tables 1 to 10 are shown in Fig. 6.2.

The squares of numbers lie on the diagonal of the chart and so we obtain the graph of $y = x^2$ from the coordinates (0,0), (1,1), (2,4), ... This is illustrated in Fig. 6.3.
[Helen Hill found the reason why the graphs on Fig. 6.2 were straight lines, and the one on Fig. 6.3 was a curve (see page 81).]

A most interesting sequence followed after two young pupils had noted from the graph of $y = x^2$ that "You can read the graph back, see 4 goes back to 2 and 16 goes back to 4." Next morning one came back very excited because an older sister had explained the meaning of the sign $\sqrt{\ }$, so they wrote down what they knew:

$$\sqrt{1} = 1,\ \sqrt{4} = 2,\ \sqrt{9} = 3,\ \sqrt{16} = 4,\ \sqrt{25} = 5.$$

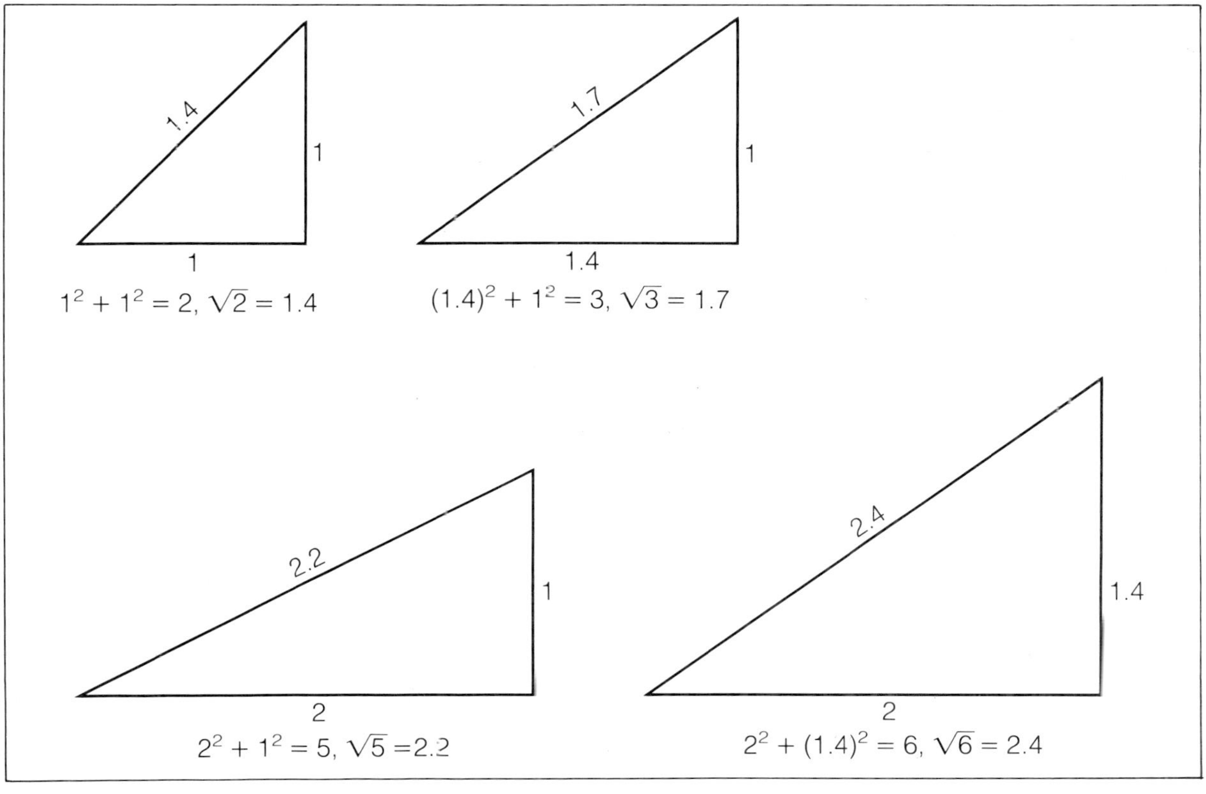

They became interested in the square roots of the 'missing' numbers 2, 3, 5, 6, etc. To find them they drew right-angled triangles with the appropriate short sides, and then measured the longest sides. Fig. 6.4 shows how they worked to find the approximate answers. They continued like this and found the square roots of other missing numbers up to 16.

Note: This was a self-imposed activity that gave them an appreciation of the value of mathematical 'shorthand', and showed that in some circumstances approximation is a practical necessity and inevitable however accurately they tried to work.

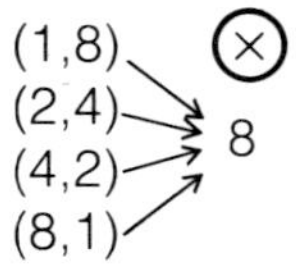

The next example is of a constant product, $xy = c$. The relevant points for $xy = 8$ are ringed on the multiplication chart (Fig. 6.1). Helen Hill uses the same form of graph in her research later (see Fig. 8.6).

The last example is given by the relation between the length of a side and the area for a rectangle of constant perimeter. Note the location of 0, 5, 8, 9, 8, 5, 0 on the multiplication chart. This is the same relation as that found by Paul Zawadjiki on page 50. (A re-read of that example could prove interesting at this point.) Secondary boys dealt with a similar situation on page 25 and graphed it as here.

Fig. 6.5 (left)

Fig. 6.6 (right)

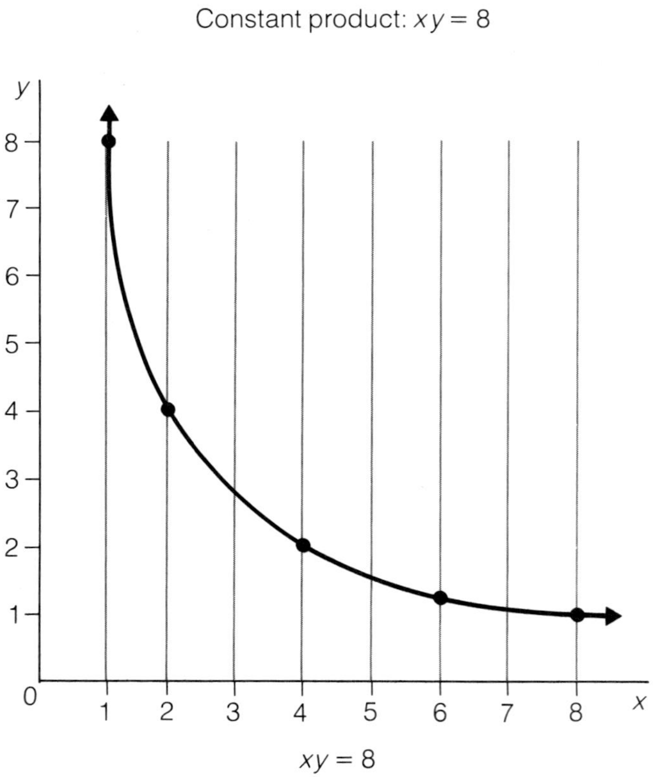

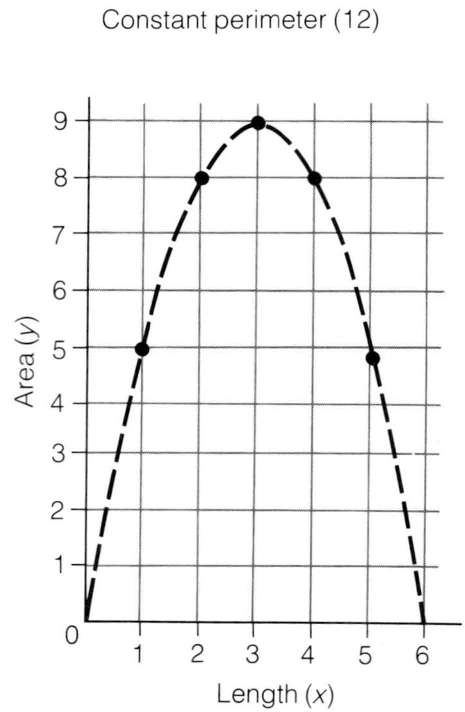

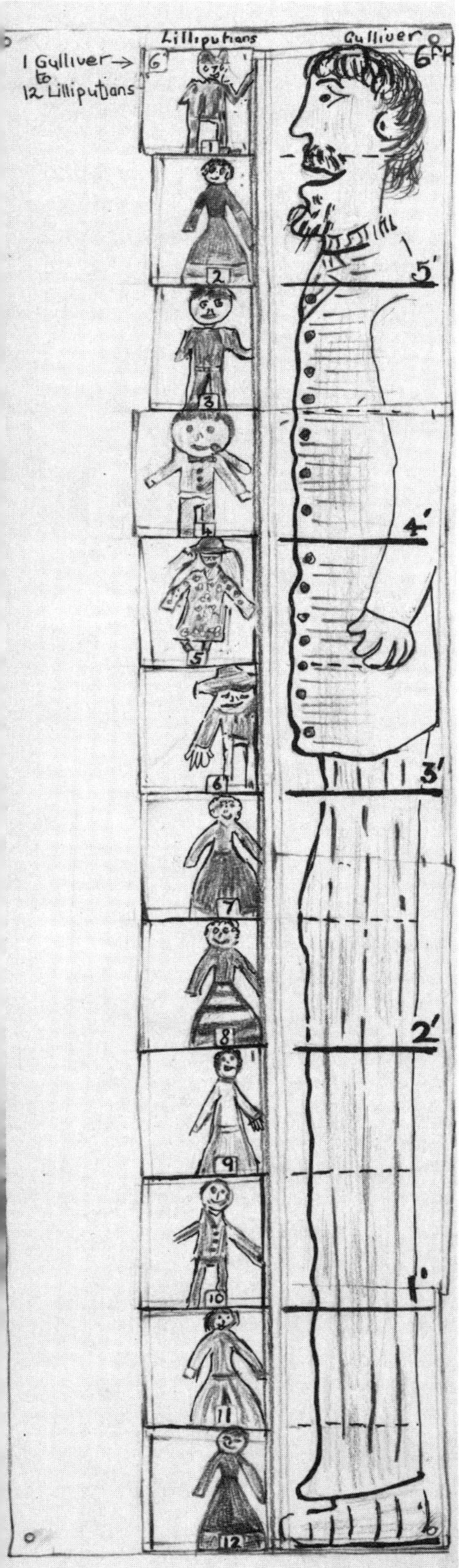

Fig. 6.7

Gulliver's Travels (a school project)

Investigations described here are based on comparison of Lilliputian size and Gulliver's size (as defined in *Gulliver's Travels*) in the context of: human statistics and heights of objects (using the relation $y = 12x$ for the conversion); bed size (using the relation $y = x^2$ for area and $12^2 = 144$ for the conversion); and food needed (using the relation $y = x^3$ for volume and $12^3 = 1728$ for the conversion). The rhyme for making Gulliver's shirt (which uses the relation $y = 2x$ in working out certain measurements) was also checked for practicability.

Three classes were involved:

(a) *class 2 (aged 8–9 years),*
(b) *class 3 (aged 9–10 years),*
(c) *class 4 (aged 10–11 years).*

The starting point was the question: *'Was Swift a good mathematician?'* This enquiry arose when class 2 (aged 8–9 years) became interested in *Gulliver's Travels,* and specifically by this remark made by Gulliver:

> *These people are most excellent mathematicians.*

It might well have gone unchallenged had not one boy said, "But it wasn't the Lilliputians who had to be good mathematicians, it was Swift who wrote it." Everyone agreed. This consensus lead to the investigation which follows It started with this class, then spread to classes of older pupils. As is usual with many projects, it crossed subject barriers.

Note: A new look at imperial units had to take place.

Class 2 (aged 8–9 years): investigating the size of Lilliputians

This class based their investigation on the statement,

> *As the common size of natives is somewhat under six inches high, so there is an exact proportion in all other animals as well as plants and trees.*

Swift's plan was grasped: he had the neat idea of turning feet to inches, so a 6 ft Gulliver would be a 6 in Lilliputian and so on. The class drew Gulliver at his actual 6 ft in height, then fitted alongside him 6 in Lilliputians: see the *reduced* sketch (Fig. 6.7). They then knew that:

1 (6 ft) Gulliver ≡ 12 (6 in) Lilliputians.

This meant that the scale was 1 in to 1 ft. A study of rulers

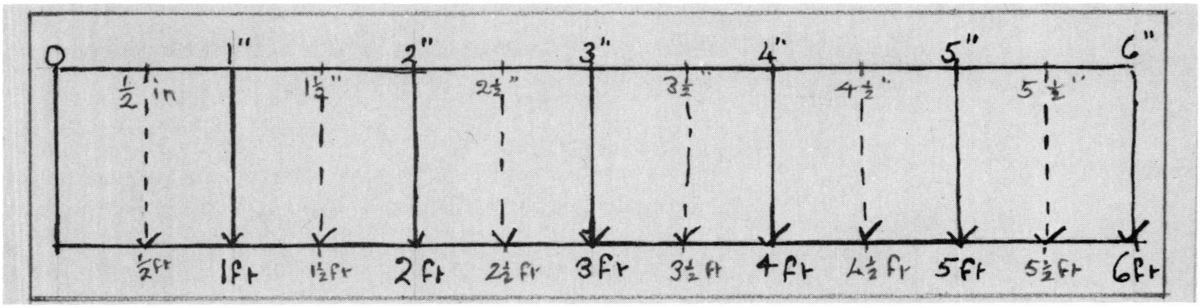
0
1"
2"
3"
4"
5"
6"
½ in
1½"
2½"
3½"
4½"
5½"
½ ft
1ft
1½ft
2 ft
2½ ft
3ft
3½ ft
4ft
4½ ft
5ft
5½ ft
6ft

Ian's Family
6in
5in
4in
3in
2in
1in
2in
Baby (can't stand up).
2ft.
Dad - 6 ft.
Mum - 5'6"
Me - 4' 3in.
By Ian

Fig. 6.8 (left)

Fig. 6.9 (lower left)

Fig. 6.10 (right)

marked in inches led to the realisation that, with this scale, it was possible to do conversions as shown in Fig. 6.9

There was no scarcity of ideas for artistic efforts. The most popular one was to draw families and/or pets the size they would be in Lilliput: a display of the former proved a focus of interest at the next parents' evening.

In the nature study period, groups selected creatures of interest to them, searched to find their average adult size, then marked that size as it would be in Lilliput (see Fig. 6.10). As illustrations give little idea of comparative sizes, they wondered if their idea could prove helpful in books. Heated discussion arose when they realised that even frogs would be less than $\frac{1}{2}$ in tall. What about fleas? Would they even be big enough to bite? Over to the entomologists!

Class 3 (aged 9–10 years): sizes and clothes for Gulliver

The news had spread and also the interest, so the teacher of class 3 suggested they go further than the young children to find out why Swift's rule worked, and discover the mathematics behind it.

They had constructed bar graphs of earlier multiplication tables, so the plan was to extend to the 12 times table (since everything in Gulliver's world was 12 times as big as in Lilliput). Using the graph (Fig. 6.11), they filled in these blanks:

$\frac{1}{12}$ of 12 = ☐	$\frac{1}{12}$ of 24 = ☐	$\frac{1}{12}$ of 36 = ☐
↓	↓	↓
$\frac{1}{12}$ of 1 ft = ☐ in	$\frac{1}{12}$ of 2 ft = ☐ in	$\frac{1}{12}$ of 3 ft = ☐ in

and so, following this pattern, obtained $\frac{1}{12}$ of 6 ft = ☐ in.

Fig. 6.11 (below) Block graph for the 12 times table

Fig. 6.12 (right) Relationship graph for 1, 2, 3 and 12 times tables

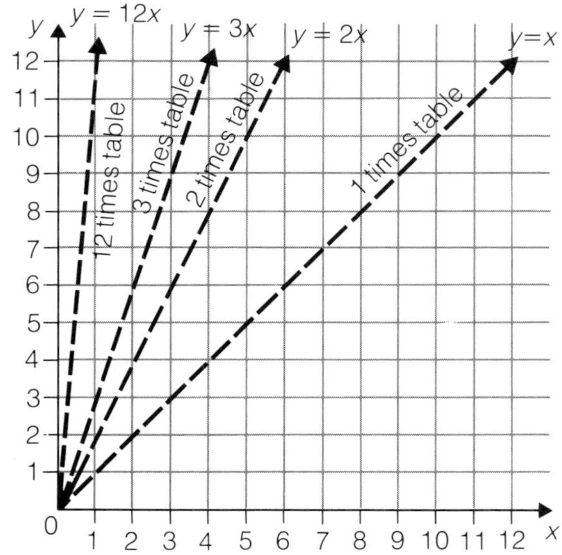

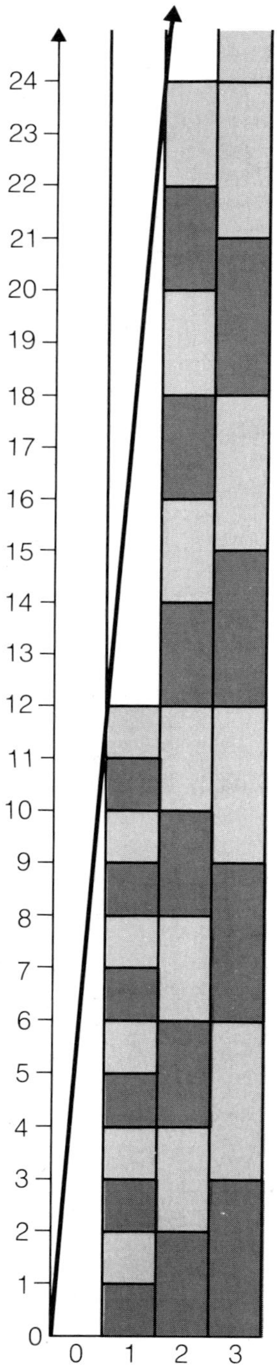

The tops of the bars were joined by drawing one straight line, and the reason for this was discussed in the context of the regular increase in length of bars. This led on to plotting the appropriate coordinates and drawing the line graphs for the following times tables (see Fig. 6.12).

1: (0,0), (1,1), (2,2), ..., (12,12)
2: (0,0), (1,2), (2,4), ..., (12,24)
3: (0,0), (1,3), (2,6), ..., (12,36)
12: (0,0), (1,12), (2,24), ..., (12,144)

(Fine grid graph paper was used to make it easier to plot the points and later to do conversions.)

Conversions

They then turned to Swift's script to note his conversions. They found one reference to capacity which was that a hogshead of wine, 'did not hold a pint'! For the rest, except for food (see class 4 later), he kept to linear (length) conversions. Here are some of his examples.

large horse:	$4\frac{1}{2}$ in,	ours $4\frac{1}{2}$ ft (pony size)
large tree:	7 ft	ours 84 ft
a sword:	3 in	ours 3 ft

The class reached the following conclusion, as expressed by Lena.

Conclusion: "So that's how Swift did his conversions. He kept mainly to what he could estimate by looking, and then generally to people. This making feet inches meant Lilliputians were $\frac{1}{12}$ of our size. It made them dwarfs like he wanted, and it was easy to calculate any heights the same way."

Gulliver's shirt

These pupils had experience of ratio in the context of $y=2x$, and were therefore ideally placed to investigate the making of Gulliver's clothes, particularly his shirt. Here is the relevant quotation from the book.

Two hundred sempstresses were employed to make me shirts ... they used cord and a ruler of an inch long. They measured my right thumb, for by a mathematical computation, that twice round my thumb is once round my wrist and so on, to the neck and waist ... they fitted me exactly.

The rule being used was as follows.

Twice round my thumb, once round my wrist,
Twice round my wrist, once round my neck,
Twice round my neck, once round my waist.

To investigate the accuracy of this rule, the children found the average measurements of six fathers, then compared those for the wrist, neck and waist with those based on the rule (ratio of 2:1). As this ratio produced a very thin neck and unbelievable waist, they tried the ratio 3:1 with results as seen in this chart.

Fig. 6.13 The Lilliputian tailors measure Gulliver for a new suit of clothes

	Thumb	Wrist	Neck	Waist
Average for fathers	3 in	7 in	14 in	33 in
Ratio 2:1	3 in	6 in	12 in	24 in
Ratio 3:1	3 in	9 in	27 in	81 in

Conclusion: "The shirt would be too tight especially round the waist for ratio 2:1 (and too baggy for 3:1)."

Gulliver's suit

The book also describes the measurements taken for a suit.

I kneeled down and they raised a ladder from the ground to my neck, and upon this ladder one of them mounted and let fall a plumb-line from my collar to the floor which just answered the length of my coat, but my waist and arms I measured myself.

Advice was sought from John's father who was a tailor. He brought in a model and showed them what measurements *should* be taken. Those for the model were

(1) centre back across $8\frac{1}{2}$ in, which is doubled to give shoulder width 17 in;
(2) collar to waist $17\frac{1}{2}$ in;
(3) sleeve length $31\frac{1}{2}$ in.

Conclusion: "Without the shoulder width, it would be just luck if it fitted."

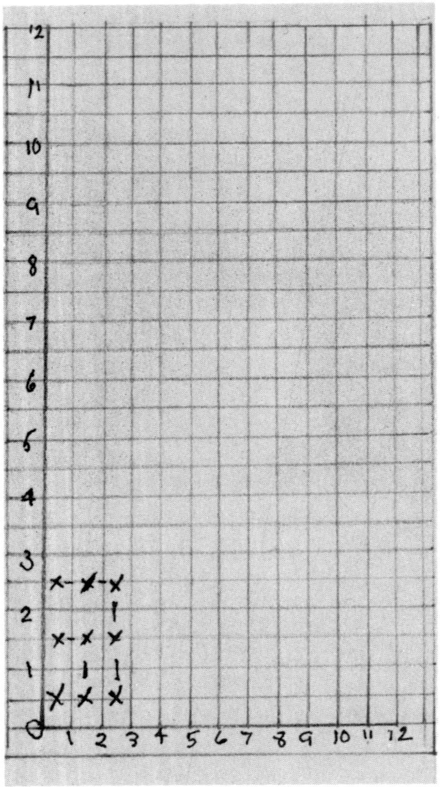

Fig. 6.14 (above) The bed

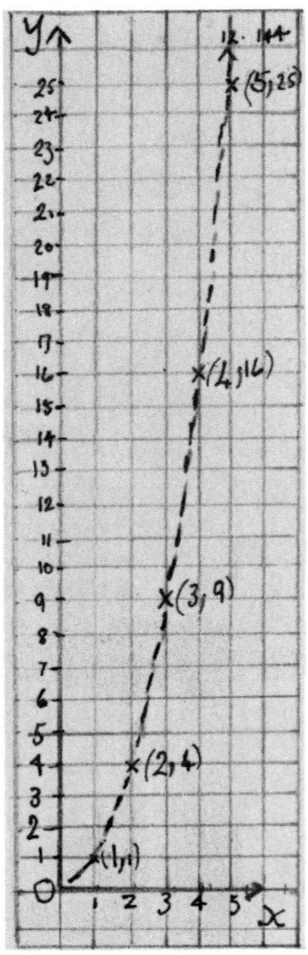

Fig. 6.15 (right) Graph of $y = x^2$

Class 4 (10–11 years): bed and food for Gulliver

Class 4 turned their attention to area and volume conversions. The book had the following to say about Gulliver's bed.

Six hundred beds of the common measure were brought in carriages and worked up in my house. An hundred and fifty of their beds sewn together made up the breadth and length, these were four double which however kept me but very indifferently from the hardness of the floor that was smooth stone.

The problem was stated by Joan Wilson as follows. "We knew $12^2 = 144$ because we had built squares on sides going up 1 unit at a time and the areas were 1, 4, 9, and to 144. But these beds aren't square. Our teacher said to try Pythagoras idea – adding on L shapes. We did it like this. You just add on the next odd number each time. The next ones will be 9+7=16, 16+9=25. The beds add on in the same way."

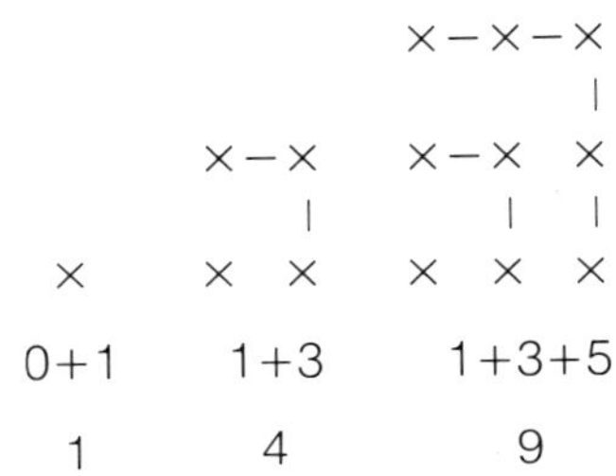

In discussion the following thoughts were raised.

(1) "Did Swift know that $12^2 = 144$ or did he think it was 150? If he did know, was he using 150 either to be on the safe side to allow for Gulliver's legs, *or* because 150×4 is easier to calculate than 144×4?"

(2) "About the depth, *four double* must mean four doubled-up if only 600 beds were used. Ours are about 6 in deep, so four would be 24 in or 2 ft. This means that four of theirs would be 2 in deep."

Conclusion: "We think 150 was a sensible estimate, but only to be 2 in deep was not practical especially on a stone floor. Swift should have tried it himself."

Next the children read about Gulliver's food.

The emperor stipulates to allow me a quantity of meat and drink sufficient for the support of 1724 Lilliputians – his mathematicians having taken the height of my body and finding it to exceed theirs in the proportion of 12 to 1, they concluded from the similarity of their bodies that mine must contain at least 1724 of theirs and, consequently, would require as much food as was necessary to support that number of Lilliputians.

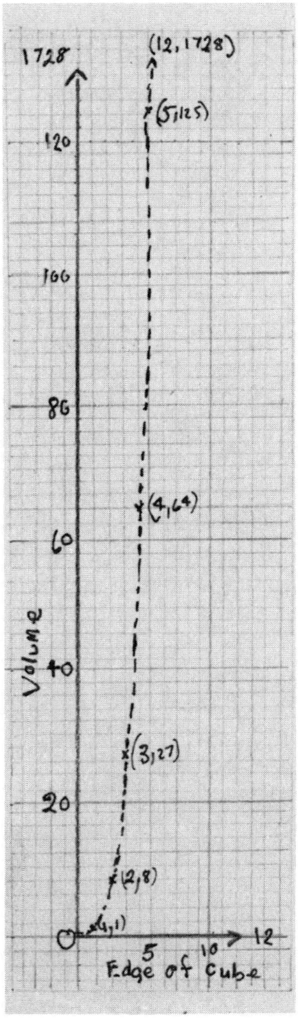

Fig. 6.16

The class thought that, in deciding on 1724, Swift had in mind 12^3 which is like thinking of a body as made up of cubes with sides of 1 unit, but, if so, the answer should be 1728. They proved it like this:

Length of edge of cube in units	Volume of cube in cubic units	Ordered pairs (coordinates)
	$y = x^3$	
1	1	(1,1)
2	8	(2,8)
3	27	(3,9)
4	64	(4,64)
5	125	(5,125)
6	216	(6,216)
⋮	⋮	
12	1728	(12,1728)

$12^3 = 1728$ not 1724

The investigation continued.

"Does the amount a man eats increase as if you fill cubes? As there is no human being 6 in tall, we checked like this using Swift's 1724 corrected to 1728.

Way 1 Food per day for our 6 ft dads average $3\frac{1}{2}$ lb or 48 oz. Food per day for 6 in Lilliputians would be 48 oz ÷ 1728 = $\frac{1}{36}$ oz.

Way 2 Food per day for Jill's 6 in pet is $1\frac{1}{2}$ oz so for a 6 ft man it would be $1\frac{1}{2}$ oz × 1728 or 162 lb.

Neither answer makes sense. Also take Alan (3 ft). His mum weighed his food for a day – $1\frac{1}{2}$ lb approx. With Swift's rule that is for a 6 ft man $1\frac{1}{2} \times 8 = 12$ lb".

Conclusion: "We don't think Swift's idea was practical. Our mums say that we boys often eat more than our dads. A visitor suggested that surface area could be a better choice than volume as a baby has more of it than a man by comparison."

(Helen Hill investigated this relationship (volume versus surface area) in her research into graphs: see Chapter 8.)

7 Spatial and numerical interactions

This chapter illustrates, as the title indicates, the part played by the unification of spatial and numerical properties in developing mathematical awareness. The topics of interest here are *properties of regular polygons* and *finding heights*.

It is interesting to note the interaction of linguistics and mathematics. In order to exemplify this valuable interaction, I offer here verbatim copies of reports written by pupils. They describe the purpose of the activity, the activity itself and conclusions drawn.

Properties of regular polygons

This research exemplifies the part played by recognition of pattern (a major factor in research). Symmetry (introduced in Chapter 4) plays a major role.

First each child made the basic apparatus of three-, four-, five- and six-sided polygons in card by drawing round plastic models and cutting them out. The plan was to extend what they discovered to other polygons, up to 360-sided, using pattern. The discoveries of the various groups are described below.

Fig. 7.1

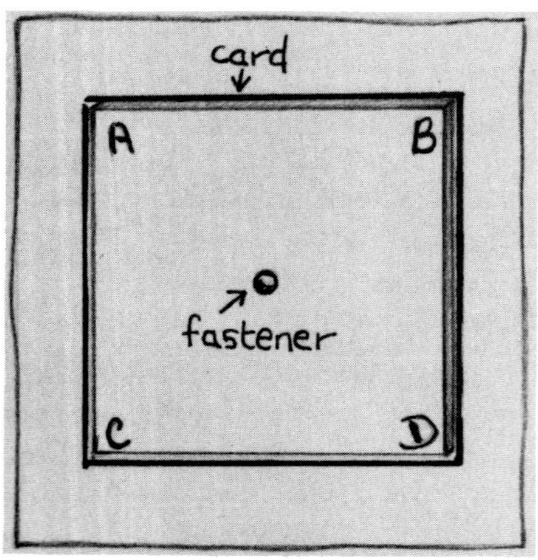

All groups: Rotate to find the properties of sides and angles

"We fixed each polygon on card with a paper fastener through its centre and marked angles A, B, C . . . as needed. We drew round it, marked angles to match those on the card, then we turned our shape round with the paper fastener – watching the fit of the angles and sides."

Conclusion: "By rotating the regular polygons in their frames we found out that all the angles of a polygon are equal and so are the sides." (*Jennifer*)

Group 1: Fold to find the number of axes

"Folding is easy. You must be careful not to count both ends of an axis. We found that: the triangle has 3 axes, the square has 4 axes and the pentagon has 5 axes."

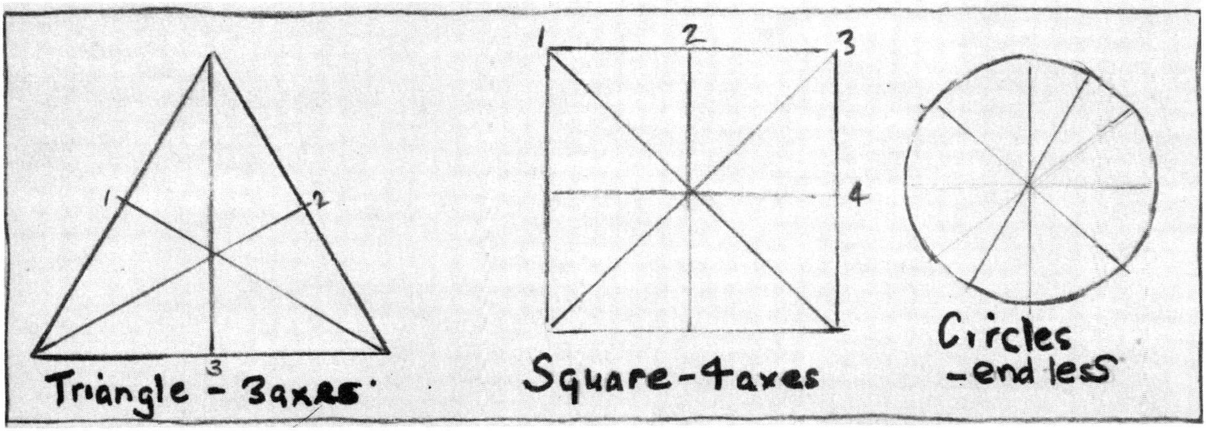

Fig. 7.2 (above)

No. of sides	Fraction of turn	No. of degrees
3	$\frac{1}{3}$	120°
4	$\frac{1}{4}$	90°
5	$\frac{1}{5}$	72°
6	$\frac{1}{6}$	60°
so 360	$\frac{1}{360}$	1°

Conclusion: "Each polygon has the same number of axes as sides, so a 360-sided polygon will have 360 axes." (*Carol*)

Group 2: Rotate to find the amount of turn needed to show rotational symmetry

"We fixed each polygon on card with a paper fastener through its centre, and rotated it in its frame as we did before to find the properties of regular polygons. This time we put angle A on the frame's A and watched how far it had to turn for the polygon to be back in its frame."

Conclusion: "Each polygon turns 360° ÷ its number of sides." (*Ruth*)

Group 3: Reflect to find the angle at the centre

"We used two joined mirrors and a ruler across like this. As you move the mirrors they make these shapes – triangle, square, pentagon and so on."

Conclusion: "The angle at the centre is 360° ÷ number of sides." (*Hilary*)

Fig. 7.3

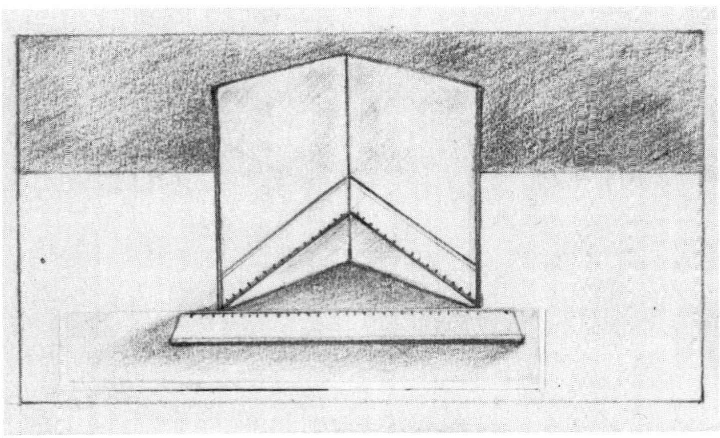

Fig. 7.4

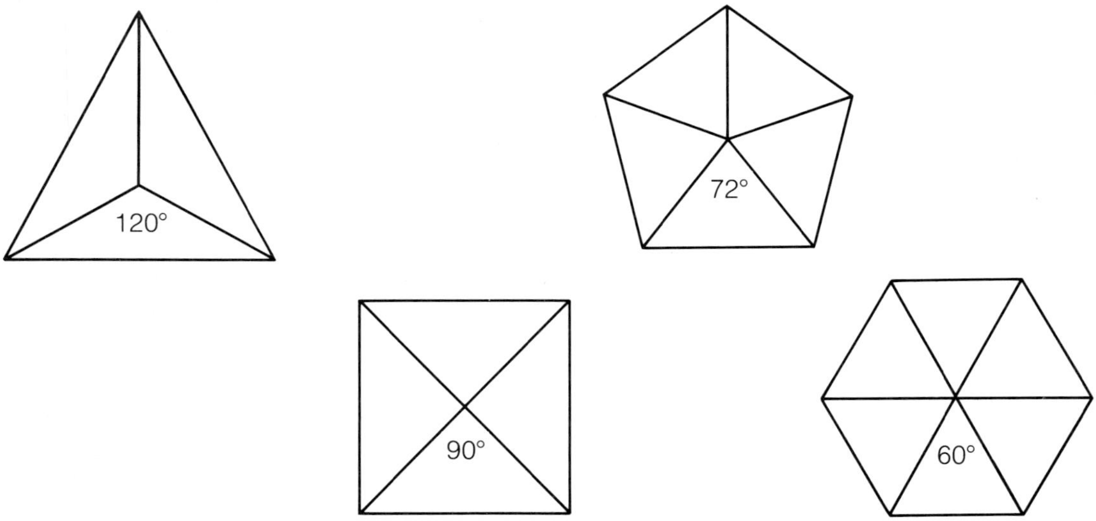

Table 7.1 Facts as we found them – look for the pattern

	Triangle	Square	Pentagon	Hexagon	By pattern 360 sides
(a) Number of sides (congruent)	3	4	5	6	... 360
Number of angles (congruent)	3	4	5	6	... 360
(b) Number of axes	3	4	5	6	... 360
(c) Rotational symmetry: fraction of a turn	$\frac{1}{3}$	$\frac{1}{4}$	$\frac{1}{5}$	$\frac{1}{6}$	... $\frac{1}{360}$
(d) Angle at the centre (fraction of 360°)	$\frac{1}{3}$	$\frac{1}{4}$	$\frac{1}{5}$	$\frac{1}{6}$	... $\frac{1}{360}$ or 1°

Then a class discussion took place (I was invited to be present), and each group leader described her own group's particular findings. A framework like the one in Table 7.1 had already been prepared, and results in turn were entered.

Finding heights

These investigations require a conceptual understanding of similarity (see the chart showing course structure, page 20). This can be established as a follow-up to congruency, comparing, for example, attribute blocks of the same shape and size for congruency, and the same shape but different size for similarity.

Consider the graph $y=x$.

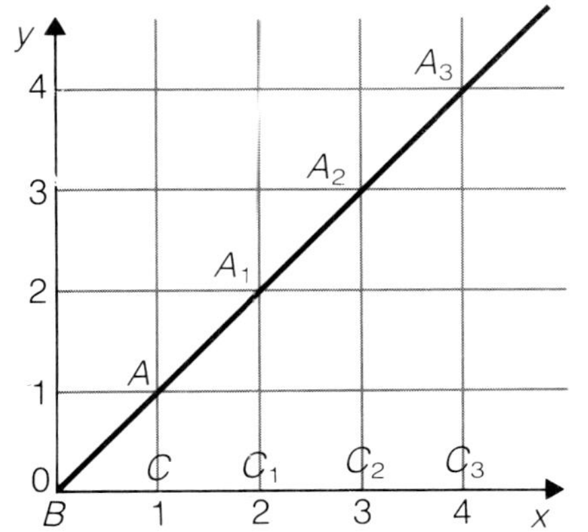

The triangles ABC, A_1BC_1, A_2BC_2 and A_3BC_3 are similar

$$\frac{\text{Opposite side}}{\text{Adjacent side}} = \frac{1}{1} \text{ [Gradient 1 in 1]}$$

Angle of elevation = 45°

(Relate to the 45° set square)

Fig. 7.5 (above)

Fig. 7.6 (right)

The extension to understanding of gradients and angles of elevation can be effected through reference to the graphical representation of $y=x$ to $y=10x$ as is shown in Fig. 7.5, for $y=x$.

Here are some examples (from older pupils). The explanations are offered verbatim.

The set square method

"The apparatus involved are a 45° set square fixed with a plumbline to the edge of the set square, and a tape measure." (*Afted Ahmad*).

Account by Karen Johnson and Amanda Flint

"Sight the top of the tree along the side of the set square opposite the right angle. Then measure the distance of the person from the tree and add the height of that person on to that distance.
Distance from tree is 3 m so $C'B'$ is 3 m
Amanda's height is $1\frac{1}{2}$ m so height of tree is $4\frac{1}{2}$ m.
Other examples from school:
(1) Height of school is 22.7 m
(2) Lamp post near staffroom is 9.40 m." (*Karen*)

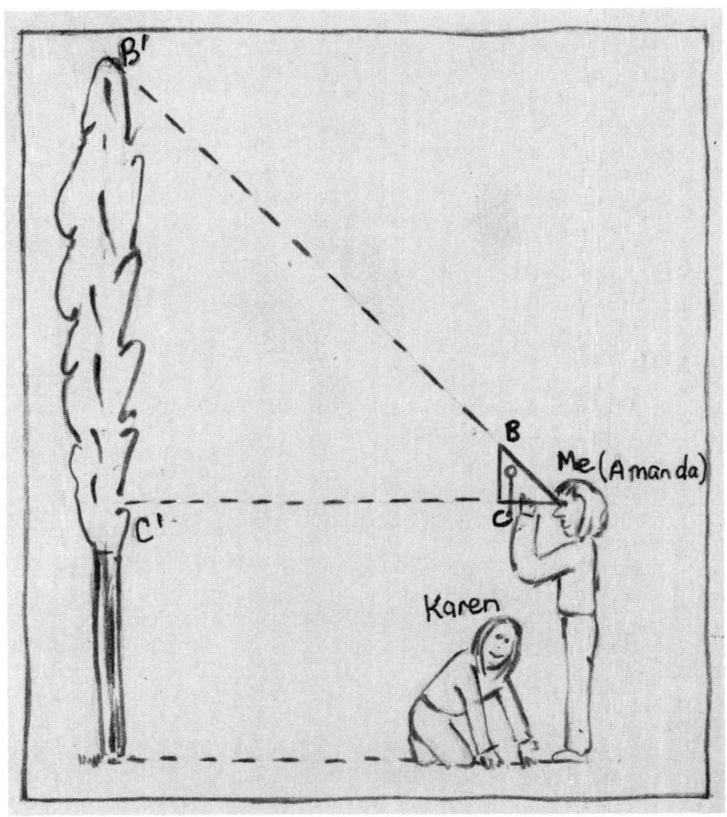

An account of how Sagheer Khan used a 1:2 set square to find the height of a bank follows.

"To measure height:

Step 1 Stand at an efficient distance from the object (bank).

Step 2 Look straight up at the object by lining the hypotenuse of the set square with the top of object – making sure that the plumbline is parallel to side of the set square.

Step 3 Get your partner to measure the distance from the object to your foot (x metres).

Step 4 Half the distance (x metres) to find A'. Add h, your height from eye to foot." (*Sagheer*)

Fig. 7.7

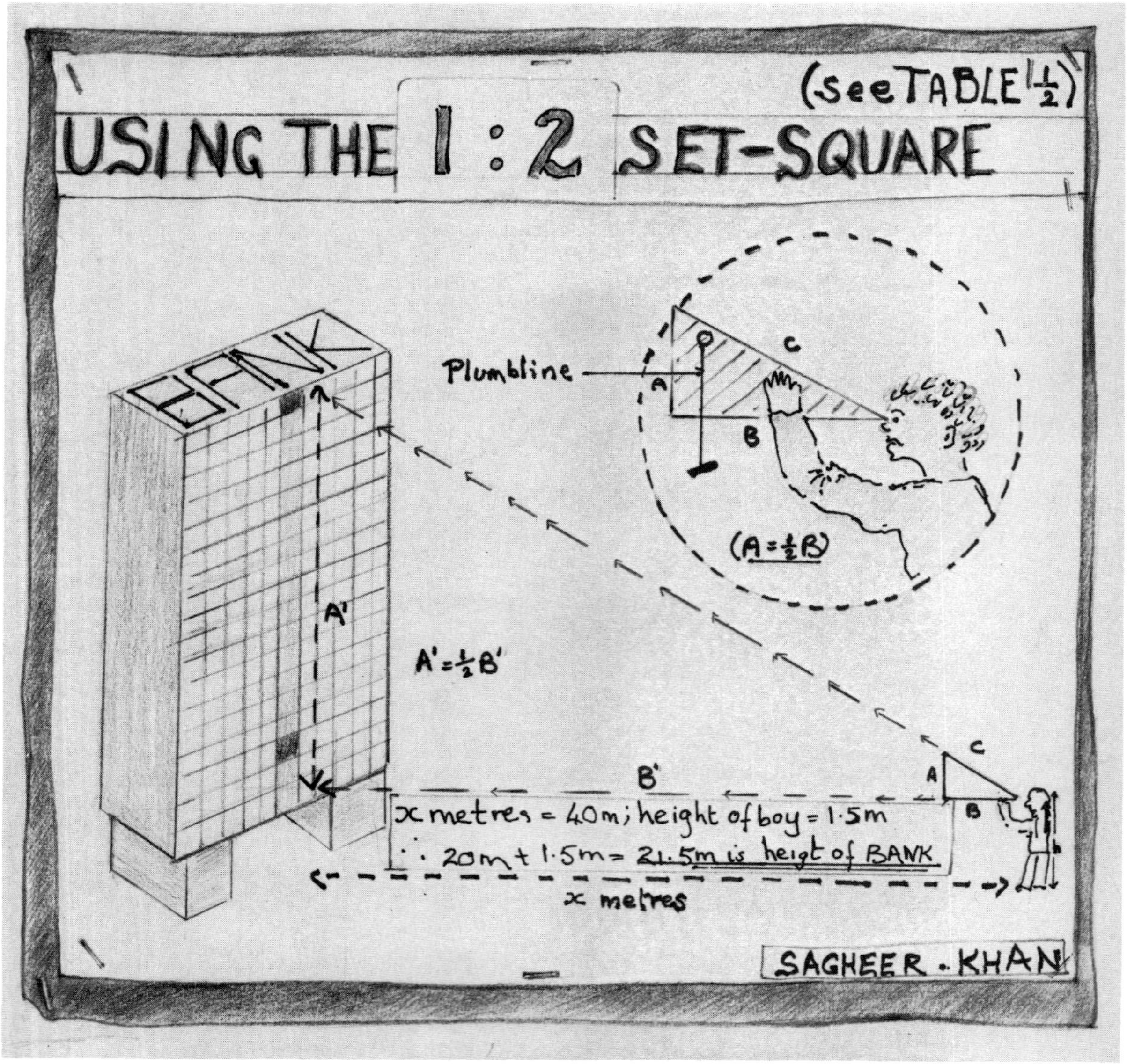

Fig. 7.8

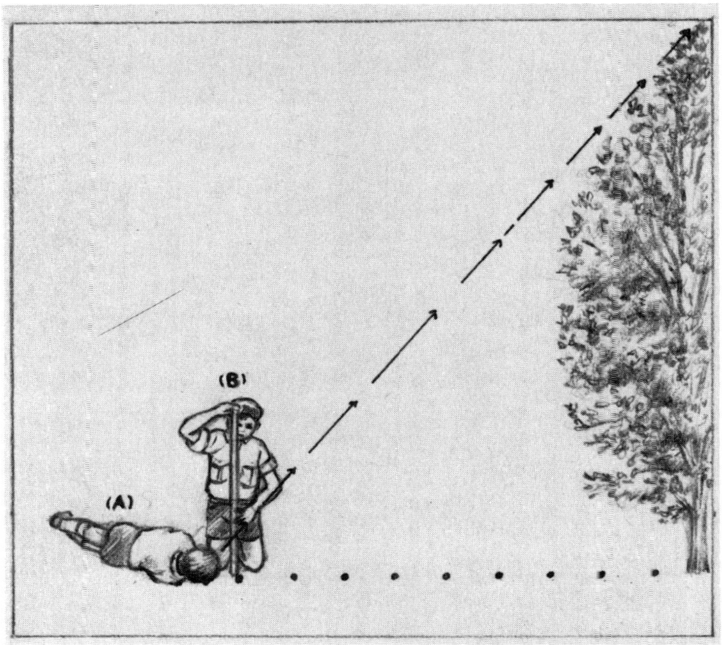

Fig. 7.9

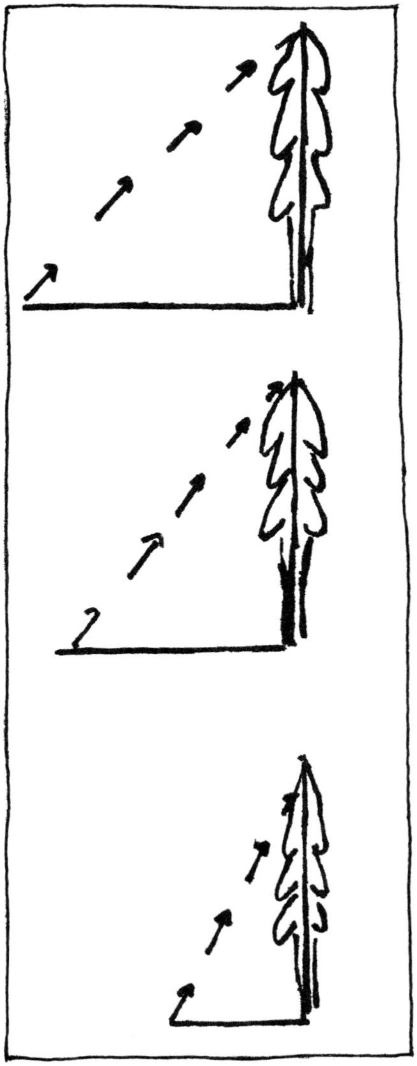

The scout method

At one time the transfer was from inches to feet. Now, since metrication, the transfer is from decimetres to metres and so aligns with the 10 times table ($y=10x$). The account is by two scouts aged 11 years.

"We take 10 paces from the tree, I lie down (like A) at the 10th pace and view the top of the tree. Tom (like B) kneels down at the 9th pace and draws his hand up the metre ruler till it cuts my view-line. The cut was at $5\frac{1}{2}$ decimetres so the tree is $5\frac{1}{2}$ metres tall approx. (ratio 1 : 10, like the paces). Other heights found were:
Wall 8.30 m and Tree $20\frac{1}{2}$ m." (*John and Tom*)

(Note how inherent in these activities is the concept of similarity.)

The shadow method

"We took one tree first. We worked out its height when the shadow from a metre stick was

1st: 1 metre at 10 a.m.
2nd: $\frac{3}{4}$ metre at 11 a.m.
3rd: $\frac{1}{2}$ metre at about noon.

The shadows actually moved to point different ways, not the same way as in the drawing. We then saw that you need not wait for these lengths. You can fit any length metre shadow into the tree shadow and the tree will be that number high in metres. It's an easy way if the sun shines. We couldn't do any more. *The sun never shone again for 6 weeks, till we broke up.*" [TRUE – June/July 1980] (*Jennifer and Jill*)

I once visited a math/nature weekend in Florida. Two boys (aged 10 years) wondered how high the trees were. I asked if they had a metre ruler – no! I told them I was $1\frac{1}{2}$ metres tall, and gave them a hint to look at my shadow. They looked, thought, then they measured my shadow in strides. They kept the same stride to measure the shadow of a tree, worked out its height, and estimated the heights of trees around. The forester told me that is the way foresters work. He was impressed by the boys.

The anglemeter method

"Bill and I made our own anglemeter like this. The black board protractor helped us to draw the semi-circle and mark out the angles. They go from 0° to 90° as you can see. We first found the height of a lamp post, then a tree. We changed over jobs for the tree.

I stood back until I could sight the top of the tree through the eyelet screws. Then Bill measured my distance from the tree and came across to see what the angle was on the anglemeter. We did a scale drawing using the distance from the tree and the size of the angle. We then worked out the height of the tree." (*Alice*)

[A good introduction to tangents of angles.]

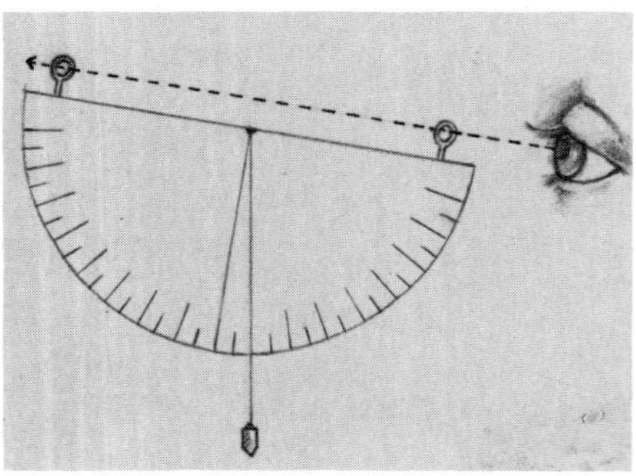

Fig. 7.10 (above)

Fig. 7.11 (right)

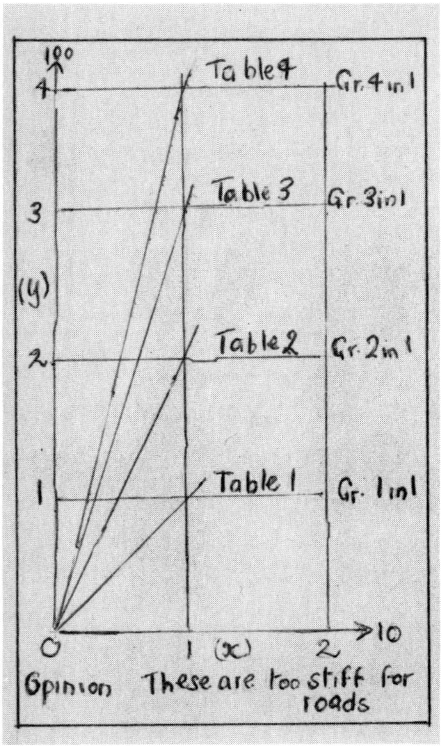

Fig. 7.12 (above)

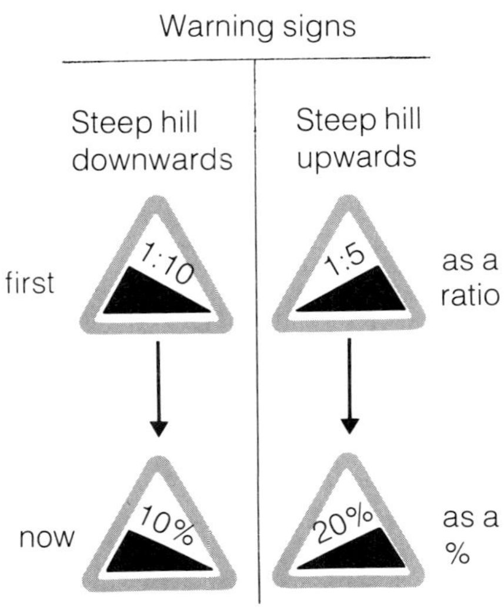

From table gradients to road gradients

As explained in the introduction to this section, a gradient is expressed as the relationship between *the opposite side of the angle of elevation and the adjacent side.* The transfer to road gradients was made by pupils aged 10–11 years.

Stage 1: Table gradients

They drew graphs as shown in Fig. 7.12 for times tables 1 to 4 with the same scale on *x* and *y* axes. Then they wrote the ratios for opposite side to adjacent side (*y*:*x*) for each one, for example:
table 2: (2:1), (4:2), (6:3), ... ratio 2:1 (constant).

They then knew that, however far the incline is extended, the gradient remains constant.

Stage 2: Road gradients (less than 1 in 1)

They found two kinds of warning signs. A helpful letter from the Transportation Department explained the reason as follows: 'Signs which previously referred to a gradient of say, 1 in 5 (indicating that the incline either rises or falls by one measure vertically for every five measures horizontally) are *now* amended to read 20%.'

For their practical work they kept to the first way. They drew the gradients separately and then combined them (see Fig. 7.13 on p. 72). Once this had been explained to me (their visitor), then came the exciting part, namely to take me to the room next door and show me the apparatus which the class had set up to time model cars moving down a slope. Kelly Smith and Shalud Iqbul were chosen to explain what happened. First they took up their positions for working it as shown in Fig. 7.14: Kelly as starter, and Shalud as timer.

Next they explained why the rougher plank was used as a runway and where the starting line was on the plank so that timings of *all* gradients were done over the same distance. Then they showed me how the intervals on the floor were spaced the same distance apart as the height of the block and how to move the block to change the gradient. Finally they tested each one of the models with Shalud giving me a personal lesson on how to use the stop-watch. I timed the last one! We then returned to report to the rest of the class.

The next stage was to give me as a present these drawings (by the 'class artist') of the model cars, and a list of timings taken by different pairs in the class, with averages. A graph of average times per gradient followed and finally a report by those responsible for the trials (Figs. 7.15 and 7.16).

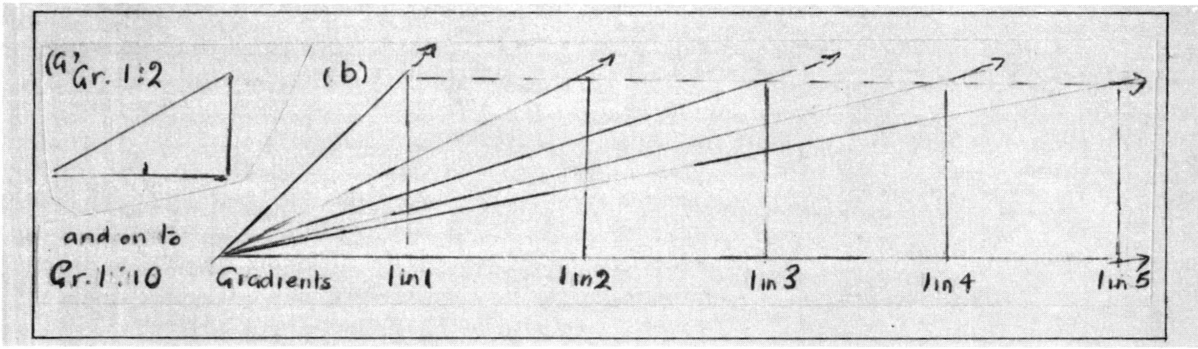

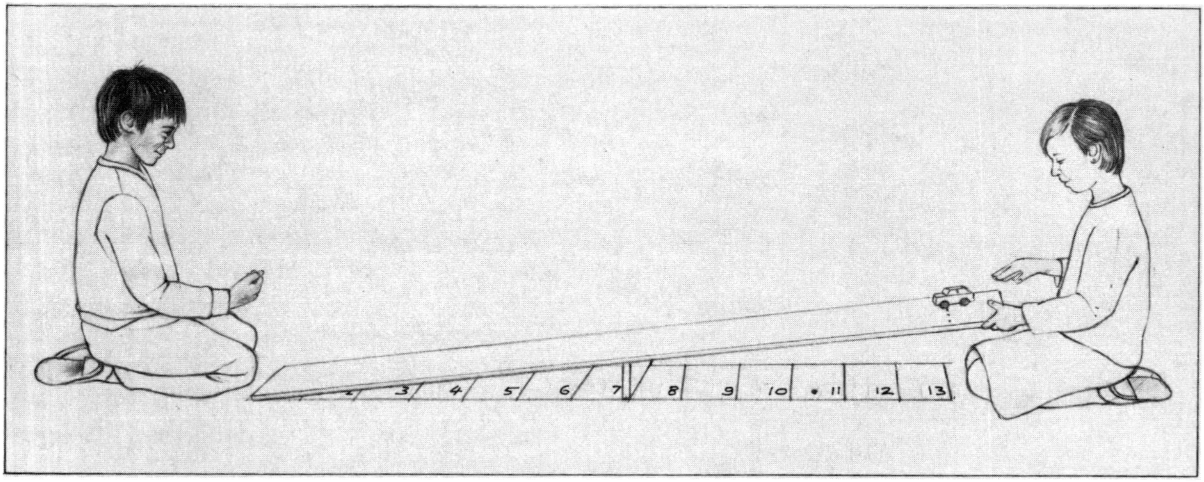

Fig. 7.13 (top)

Fig. 7.14 (above)

Fig. 7.15 (right)

Table 7.2 Times (averages for a number of timings per car)

Gradient	1:12	1:10	1:8	1:6	1:4
Tank	5 sec	4 sec	$2\frac{1}{2}$ sec	$1\frac{3}{4}$ sec	$1\frac{1}{4}$ sec
Mustang	$2\frac{1}{2}$ sec	$2\frac{1}{4}$ sec	2 sec	$1\frac{1}{2}$ sec	1 sec
Capri	$2\frac{1}{2}$ sec	$2\frac{1}{2}$ sec	$2\frac{1}{4}$ sec	$1\frac{1}{4}$ sec	1 sec
'Banger'	$2\frac{3}{4}$ sec	2 sec	$2\frac{1}{2}$ sec	$1\frac{3}{4}$ sec	$1\frac{1}{4}$ sec
Average (approx.)	$3\frac{1}{4}$ sec	$2\frac{3}{4}$ sec	$2\frac{1}{4}$ sec	$1\frac{1}{2}$ sec	$1\frac{1}{4}$ sec

Fig. 7.16 (below)

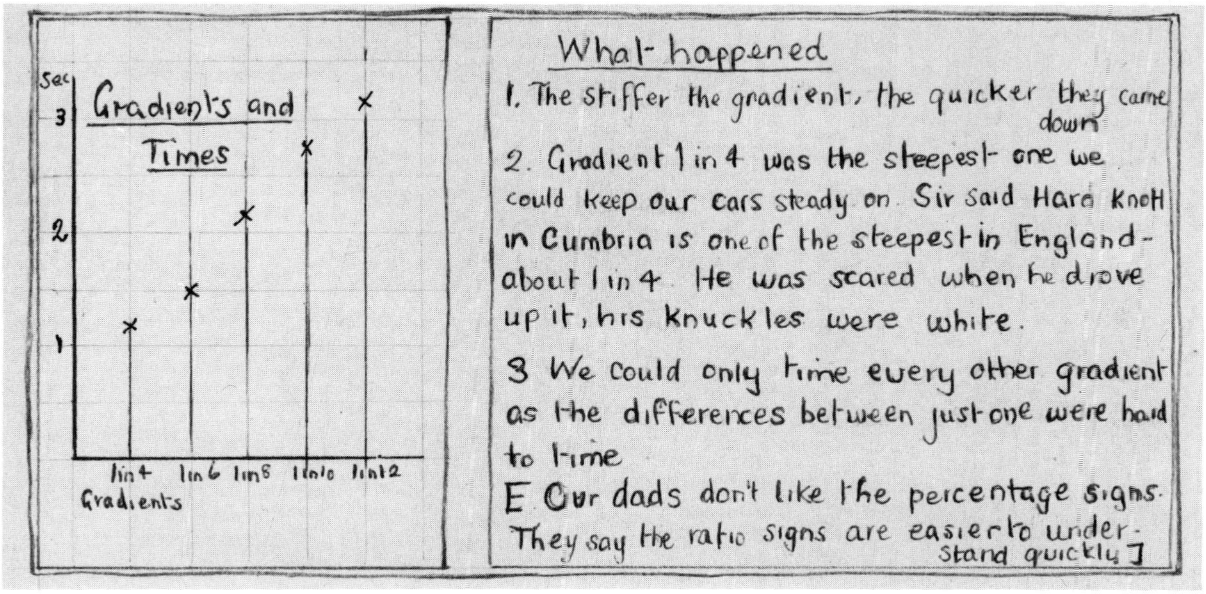

I have offered this example of research because, in my opinion, it exemplifies what can be achieved by a problem-solving approach based on reasoning. Had these children been conditioned to instrumental learning, i.e. rote practice, they would have been hard-pressed not only to explain each stage, but also to connect the stages in their search for a conclusion. It was of interest to me how naturally they were able to explain their several contributions. You will not be surprised to hear that their teacher, who of course planned the whole research, adopts this reasoning approach in all subject areas – the children are conditioned to it. Surely such training should help counteract the all-too-frequent criticism that older students seem to have given up efforts to think, and instead search for rules to follow (described to me by a trainer at a well-known research centre as those 'human robots'). It is understandable that a reasoning attitude cannot be turned on suddenly as required; it needs rather to be fostered from an early age.

I cannot leave this chapter, with its interest in angles, without including another activity that is always popular, namely, the construction of a right-angle with knotted rope.

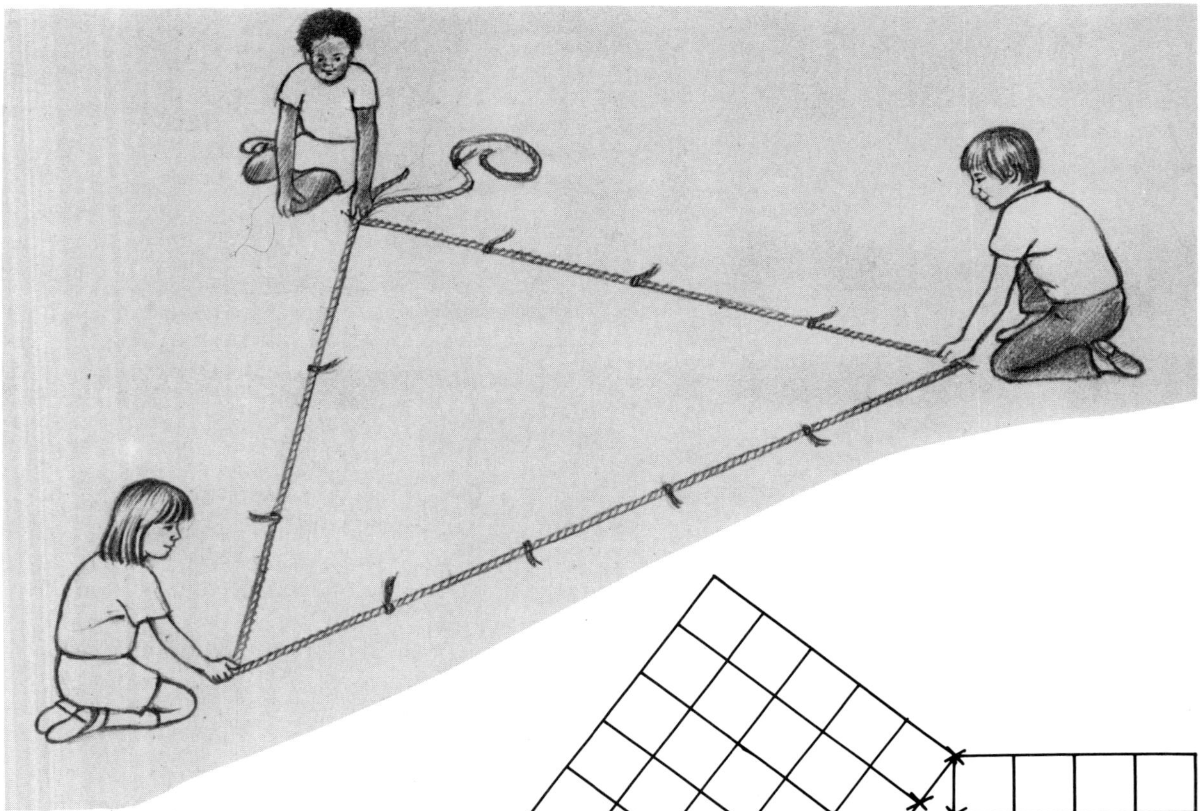

Fig. 7.17 (above)

Fig. 7.18 (right)

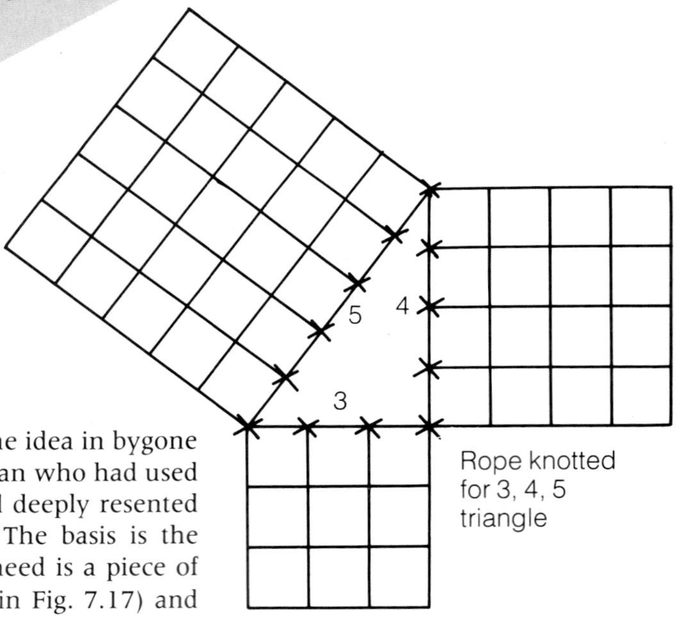

Rope knotted for 3, 4, 5 triangle

Egyptian rope-stretchers supposedly used the idea in bygone ages. I met, only the other day, a groundsman who had used it all his life when marking out pitches and deeply resented the 'new-fangled' ways now being used. The basis is the Pythagorean trio 3, 4, 5. All the children need is a piece of rope knotted in equal intervals (as shown in Fig. 7.17) and three pegs. *The problem is to make a right-angle.* This can give them a lead into $3^2 + 4^2 = 5^2$ (see Fig. 7.18).

It was this experience, as he explains himself, which inspired John Searjeant's imaginative research into square numbers, and finally to generate the rule for factoring the difference of two squares (see Chapter 8): from knotted rope to $x^2 - y^2 = (x-y)\ (x+y)$!!

8 Pupils with initiative showing creative reasoning

Examples from previous chapters

As the specific examples which follow are from older juniors (aged 10–11 years), I am starting with some examples which have already cropped up, with younger children.

As a first example take Tim (aged $7\frac{1}{2}$ years), and his reaction to difference (page 12). His immediate response was, "If you halve the strips, you just halve the differences. . . Halve and halve for ever . . . – it [the difference] never ends but it's there." Tim has, at so young an age, the ability to extend beyond the concrete to the infinite. What reasoning! He brought a snap of his family and an enlargement of it next day to show Paul. "Now think of it getting smaller and smaller", he said to Paul. The bell went, and Paul shot off, but kindly Dawn edged round, "Your mummy is pretty", she said consolingly. (Yet note how she coped in the supermarket (page 43) – no infinite there!) A similar imaginative leap forward was made by another Paul when he reduced Brian to tears by destroying his goal of counting to a million (page 89). "You can go on to a million and one can't you?" he replied dismissively. And why did Brian cry? I think because he knew that this was true – there is no end! What adult planning could have achieved this awareness? As a final example, I refer to the research on the multiplication chart done by the older boy, Paul Zawadjiki (page 50). The teacher rang me up. I went to visit that day. Paul's sense of pattern was amazing – his logical pursuance of it astonishing. Yet this boy, I was told, scarcely spoke in class because he was sensitive to his linguistic handicap. Not so when explaining his own thoughts; in that situation he was most literate!

What about, you may well say, when children's initiatives can be judged as wrong in the context of adult thinking? Obviously dismissal on that ground could stifle potential for creative thinking, and hence destroy the contribution that children's ideas make to their learning. I would offer as a personal opinion that the onus lies on the teacher to make a swift appraisal of the cause of a seemingly non-mathematical idea. Could it be sheer thoughtlessness, lack of mathematical background, or indeed immaturity? Take, for example, the pupils in the Goliath example who turned down the visiting mathematician's idea of halving Goliath and then David. "And make David wrong too", said the leader, "No". The teacher read this as an indication that, later (not immediately since this would douse their enthusiasm and pride), ratio needed to be studied. Would you agree? One other redress is also open, namely selfcorrection. In John Searjeant's account which follows (page 78) you will read how an initiative, pursued at the age of 9 years, was re-examined two years later, and led to a corrected and correct conclusion (he moved from factoring the difference of two squares $x^2 - y^2$ as $x + y$ to $x^2 - y^2 = (x + y)\ (x - y)$).

This leads me into the following three examples of self-inspired individual research by older juniors. All three children, when faced later with the 11+ examination (now happily almost extinct) which decided whether they would move into selective or non-selective secondary schools, passed with ease into the former and later went to university. The two boys – but not the practical Helen – had to be warned not to go off on some investigation of their own, but to concentrate on the examination paper.

Individual examples from older juniors

A short summary is now offered of each pupil's research to clarify in advance what motivated each of them. Please do not be deterred if their approach is not one that is prescribed as accepted procedure in text-books!

John's research

The inspiration (as explained by John) came from a classroom discussion on Egyptian rope-stretchers, and how they used the 3, 4, 5 trio to produce a right-angled triangle. His class watched the groundsman use it, then tried it themselves (Fig. 7.17).

The following resumé was offered when John's work was reproduced for the *Madison Project* (Director Professor Robert Davis) in *The Journal of Children's Mathematical Behaviour* (U.S.A.).

John began his work by looking at what he called 'square numbers', e.g. 25 = 16 + 9. He found several trios of square numbers which could be used as lengths of sides of right triangles; and from this point, he began investigating number patterns which emerged from his chart of square numbers. Two years later John conducted a follow-up study in which he discovered an error he had *made in his earlier report. His analysis of this error, and subsequent re-analysis of his data, led him to generate the rule for factoring the difference of two squares [$x^2 - y^2 = (x + y)(x - y)$]. ... The paper is presented here as a fascinating example of a creative young mind at work.*

Helen's research

The graphs in Chapter 6 were the basis for this work. Helen's research was directed to finding out:

(a) whether the form of a graph (straight or curved) could be foretold by a study beforehand of the kind of sequence to be graphed;

(b) the relationship of volume to surface area evoked by the conclusion in the food part of the Gulliver project (p. 63).

It is interesting that she moved on in (a) to looking at x^4, and in (b) to graphing A/V (a graph new to her).

Peter's research

The graphs in Chapter 6 and work on angles of elevation in Chapter 7 were the basis for this work. It would be difficult to report Peter's pages of research as each stage was explored in depth and analysed. For this reason I have opted to offer a verbatim account as taped when Peter answered questions on the stages which finally took him into calculus – surely as rigorous a test of understanding that anyone could be asked to face! He told me afterwards that, "describing what we did for you in class was a bit difficult – but when it came to my own work, it was dead simple." So on to the 'dead simple'! To summarise, he explored the graphs of $y = x^2$, $y = x^3$ then back to $y = x$ leading, through a relevant study of gradient and area, to the following chart which contains his conclusions.

For the graph $y = x$, the slope is 1 and the area is $\frac{x^2}{2}$ *

For the graph $y = x^2$, the slope is $2x$* and the area is $\frac{x^3}{3}$ *

For the graph $y = x^3$, the slope is $3x^2$** and the area is $\frac{x^4}{4}$ *

Peter did those marked *. Trevor did the one marked **.

Individual examples from older juniors

Pythagoras presents a problem
by John Searjeant (9 years)

"In class we were discussing the Egyptian rope-stretchers. They used 3, 4, 5 measurements to make a right-angle (Fig. 7.17).

25 = 16 + 9 are square numbers

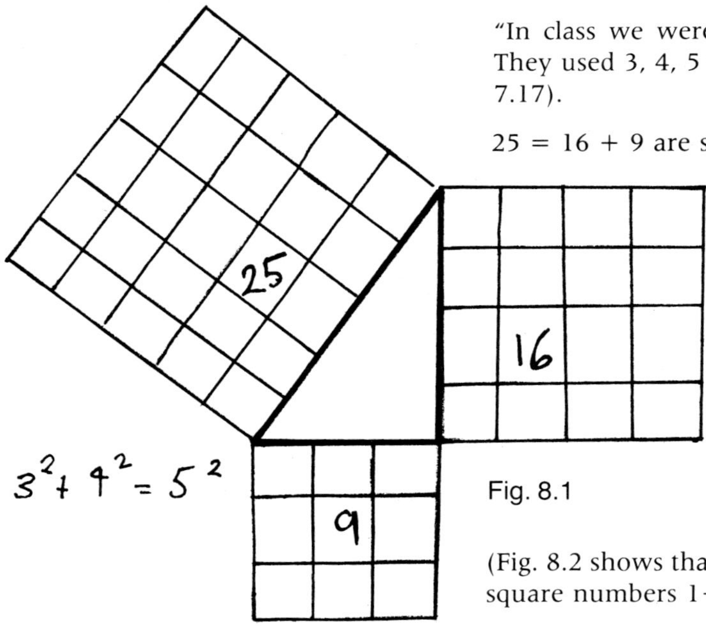

Fig. 8.1

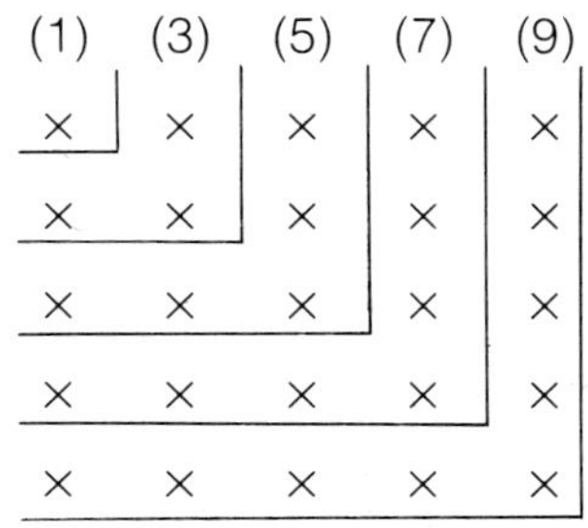

Fig. 8.2

(Fig. 8.2 shows that if you add odd numbers in order you get square numbers 1+3=4, 4+5=9, 9+7=16, 16+9= 25.)

I thought that if an odd number was a square number then I could use it like 9 here to make a right-angled triangle.

$4^2 = 16$, $5^2 = 25$ > 9 (3^2)

These are square numbers. I found them by adding on odd numbers.

Square	Difference	Square	Difference	Square	Difference
$1^2 = 1$	+3	$9^2 = 81$	+19	$17^2 = 289$	+35
$2^2 = 4$	+5	$10^2 = 100$	+21	$18^2 = 324$	+37
$3^2 = 9$	+7	$11^2 = 121$	+23	$19^2 = 361$	+39
$4^2 = 16$	+9	$12^2 = 144$	+25	$20^2 = 400$	+41
$5^2 = 25$	+11	$13^2 = 169$	+27	$21^2 = 441$	+43
$6^2 = 36$	+13	$14^2 = 196$	+29	$22^2 = 484$	+45
$7^2 = 49$	+15	$15^2 = 225$	+31	$23^2 = 529$	+47
$8^2 = 64$	+17	$16^2 = 256$	+33	$24^2 = 576$	+49
				$25^2 = 625$	

Using pattern

I then used the pattern to make up this chart. I used the numbers to be squared, *not* the squares of numbers. It goes like the 4 times table.

	1st row		2nd row		3rd row
	1^2	=	0^2	+	1^2
	5^2	=	4^2	+	3^2
	13^2	=	12^2	+	5^2
	25^2	=	24^2	+	7^2
so	41^2	=	40^2	+	9^2
	⋮		⋮		⋮
	181^2	=	180^2	+	19^2

1st row: 1 5 13 25...
4 8 12

2nd row: 0 4 12 24...
4 8 12

3rd row: 1+3=4, 3+5=8, 5+7=12....
[He carried on from 16 to 36]

Fig. 8.3 (below)

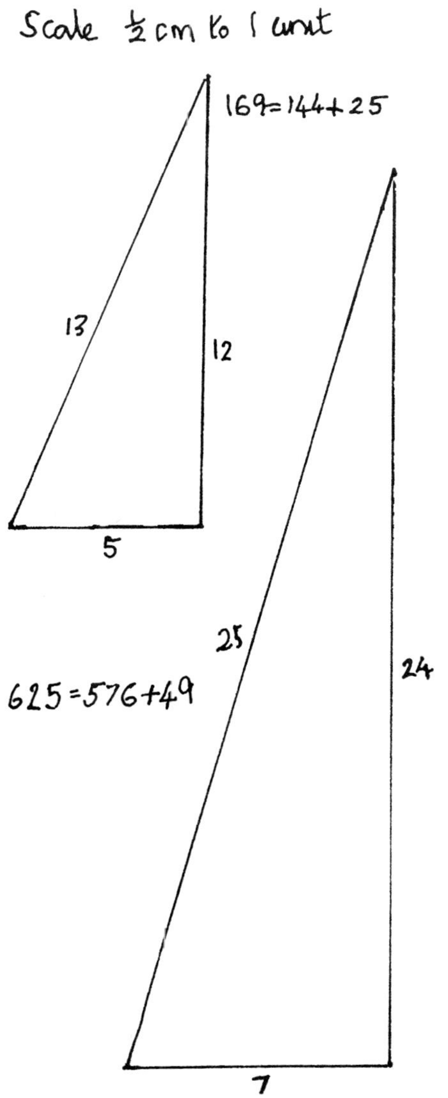

An American visitor from Chicago helped me to get the 1st trio ($1^2=0^2+1^2$). It is an exception for it doesn't make a right-angle triangle. It has no base.

It worked for $13^2 = 12^2 + 5^2$. It didn't come up again until $25^2 = 24^2 + 7^2$. (I have put a frame round them.)

These trios make the right-angled triangles shown at the left. Scale $\frac{1}{2}$ cm to 1 unit.

Now the numbers it worked with are odd square numbers. So I thought get an odd square number such as 361 and halve it making $180\frac{1}{2}$.

Take the whole number above squared $(181)^2 = 32761$
then the whole number below squared $(180)^2 = 32400$
361

Take the lower one from the top one and you will be left with a square number 361. $361 = 19^2$ and it worked.

I thought you could *not* do this with even square numbers because when you halve them you will only get one number. Thus $36 \div 2 = 18$ and 18 is the only number and you have got to have two numbers like when I halved 49 ($24\frac{1}{2}$) so I could use 24 and 25.

You have a pattern if you look at it this way. If you add the first two numbers, they will equal the last number squared."

$$25^2 - 24^2 = 7^2$$
$$25 + 24 = 49$$
$$7^2 = 49$$

(*Note*: His rule, *so far*, for the difference of two squares is $x^2 - y^2 = x + y$)

Two years later

1. "When I looked back at the work I did when I was 9 years old I could see where I was wrong. In my *Using pattern* section, I said you could not deal with even square numbers

like odd square numbers. I said $36 \div 2 = 18$. 18 is the only number and you have got to have two numbers like when I halved 49 and got $24\frac{1}{2}$ and used 24 and 25. This is where I went wrong.

I found this out by repeating what I did with an odd square number with an even square number. I followed the rule and it worked.

Example: $36 \div 2 = 18$ add and subtract $\frac{1}{2}$ leaving $18\frac{1}{2}$ and $17\frac{1}{2}$, then $18\frac{1}{2}^2 - 17\frac{1}{2}^2$ gives a difference of 6^2. I followed this up with other examples and this proved my theory.

Other examples:

$$2\tfrac{1}{2}^2 - 1\tfrac{1}{2}^2 = 2^2$$
$$8\tfrac{1}{2}^2 - 7\tfrac{1}{2}^2 = 4^2$$
$$18\tfrac{1}{2}^2 - 17\tfrac{1}{2}^2 = 6^2$$
$$32\tfrac{1}{2}^2 - 31\tfrac{1}{2}^2 = 8^2$$
$$50\tfrac{1}{2}^2 - 49\tfrac{1}{2}^2 = 10^2$$

This deals with the consecutive *even* squares of numbers 4, 16, 36, 64 and 100.

2. *Finding a rule*. When I looked at these examples I thought I could find a rule. Mrs Whittaker suggested I gave the 1st numbers a letter to stand for them all, and another letter for all the 2nd numbers. I chose x for the 1st numbers to be squared and y for the 2nd ones.

Example: $18\frac{1}{2}^2 - 17\ ^2 = 36$ and $18\frac{1}{2} + 17\frac{1}{2} = 36$

$x^2 - y^2 = 36$ and $x + y = 36$

This works for the *other examples* as well, i.e. $x^2 - y^2 = x + y$

Then I tried 6 and 3: $6^2 - 3^2 = 6 + 3$

$$36 - 9 = 9$$
$$27 = 9$$

This is wrong but 27 is 9×3 and $6 - 3$ is 3, so I need to multiply $6 + 3$ by $6 - 3$ to make $27 = 27$.

This makes the rule $x^2 - y^2 = (x + y)(x - y)$

I tried 9 and 4. It worked

$$9^2 - 4^2 = (9 + 4)(9 - 4)$$
$$81 - 16 = 13 \times 5$$
$$65 = 65$$

I tried fractions. It worked

$$2\tfrac{1}{2}^2 - 2^2 = (2\tfrac{1}{2} + 2)(2\tfrac{1}{2} - 2)$$
$$6\tfrac{1}{4} - 4 = 4\tfrac{1}{2} \times \tfrac{1}{2}$$
$$2\tfrac{1}{4} = 2\tfrac{1}{4}$$

So really $x^2 - y^2 = (x + y)(x - y)$ is always right. It is for the examples like $18\frac{1}{2}^2 - 17\frac{1}{2}^2$ because $x - y = 1$ and if you multiply by 1 it leaves the product the same, therefore it works for 1 as well."

John Searjeant (aged 11)

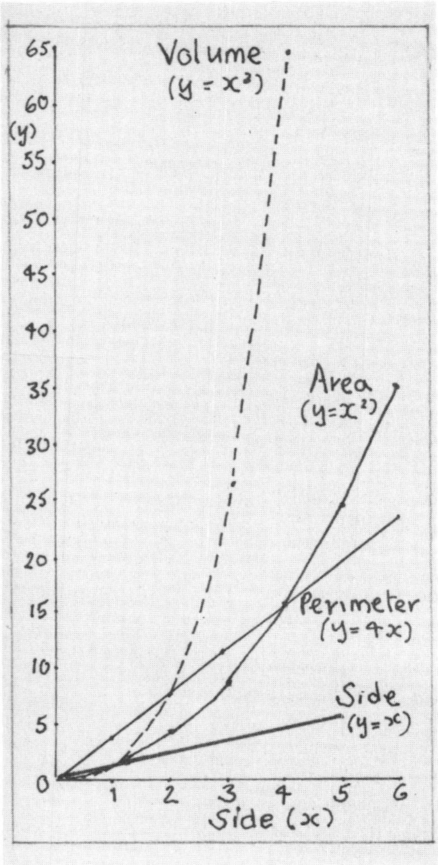

Fig. 8.4

Sequences and their graphs by Helen Hill (11 years)

Helen's group had built up cubes that fitted on squares like these.

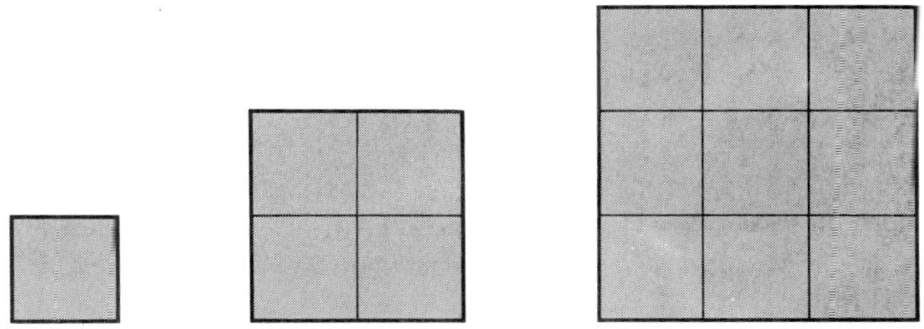

1 unit 2 units 3 units

They then built up the following sequences.

Side	0	1	2	3	4
Perimeter	0	4	8	12	16
Area	0	1	4	9	16
Volume	0	1	8	27	64

They graphed these as shown in Fig. 8.4. It was these sequences and their graphs that aroused Helen's interest. Her research (verbatim) is quoted here.

"I wondered why the graphs for $y=x$ and $y=4x$ made straight lines, and for $y=x^2$ and $y=x^3$ made curves. So I thought I would see if the way the sequences grew had anything to do with it.

I filled in this chart to help me. That day the B.B.C. came to film us.

Sides $y=x$	0 1 2 3 4 1 1 1 1
Perimeter $y=4x$	0 1 4 9 16 4 4 4 4
Area $y=x^2$	0 1 4 9 16 1 3 5 7 2 2 2
Volume $y=x^3$	0 1 8 27 64 1 7 19 37 6 12 18 6 6

First I tested the $y=x$ and $y=4x$ sequences. Each one kept the same number for its increase. They made straight-line graphs. So did the $y=2x$, and on to $y=10x$, when we graphed them for tables.

Then I checked on $y=x^2$. Its sequence goes up first in a pattern of odd numbers, then to the same number.

When I reached $y=x^3$, the camera came across to me, and my Headmaster came to question me.

'I can't see a pattern', he said about this row. 'Do it again,' I whispered. Then he saw it. Then I finished it to the same number (6).

$y=x$ takes 1 row to get to the same number for differences, $y=x^2$ takes 2 rows, $y=x^3$ takes 3 rows. I guessed $y=x^4$ takes 4 rows. I tested it and it does (24). I think the rule is that if you add on the same number in a sequence you get a straight line, but if you multiply like squaring and cubing here – you get a curve."

[In mathematical language an arithmetic sequence leads to a straight line and a geometrical to a smooth curve known as an exponential curve.]

The volume of cubes (x^3) and their surface area ($6x^2$)

Helen first filled in the table then drew the graphs. She was delighted that $6x^2$ made a curve as this followed her rule.

Then once again Helen pursued her own line of research, promoted by the statement and consequent query written on her own graph. Her opinion was offered as follows.

Fig. 8.5

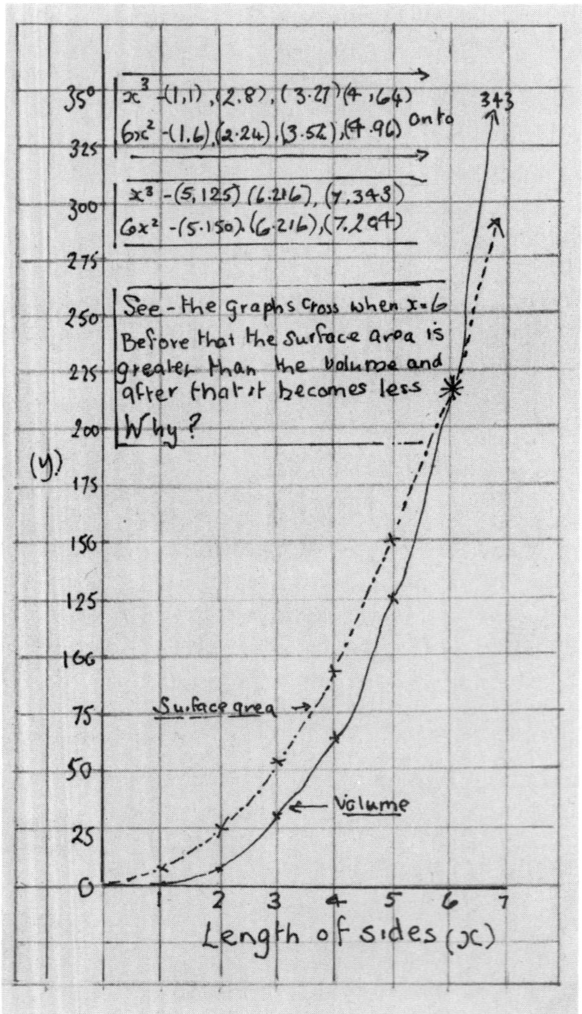

"I thought about it for a week. It must be due to a cube having 6 faces.

(a) That could explain why they meet on a side of 6 for 6 is common to both.
Yes because V. $= 6^2 \times 6 = 216$
S.A. $= 6^2 \times 6 = 216$

(b) But when the sides are under 6 say 4, then V. $= 4^2 \times 4$
S.A. $= 4^2 \times 6$
so surface area should be above.

(c) And when they are over 6 say 7, then V. $= 7^2 \times 7$
S.A. $= 7^2 \times 6$

so volume would be above.
Yes – that's right." (*Helen*)

Side	Area ($6x^2$)	Volume (x^3)	$A \div V$
1	6	1	6
2	24	8	3
3	54	27	2
4	96	64	$1\frac{1}{2}$
5	150	125	$1\frac{1}{5}$
6	216	216	1
12	864	1728	$\frac{1}{2}$

Fig. 8.6 (right)

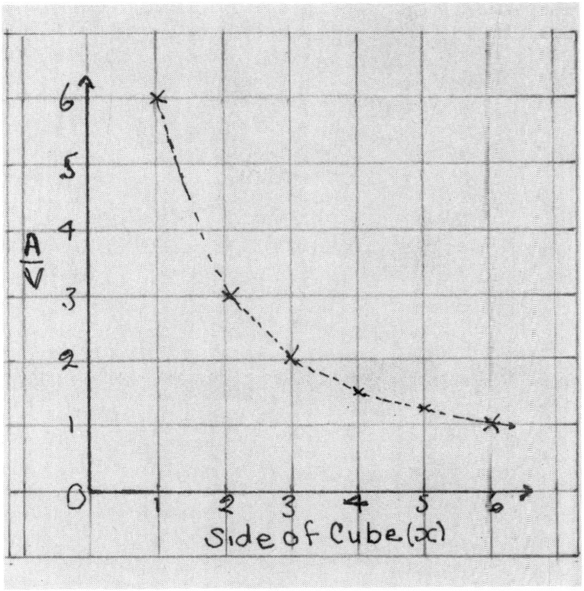

She then turned her attention to what would happen if she divided the surface area ($y=6x^2$) by the volume ($y=x^3$): knowing Helen I guessed that a graph was in mind! Here is her table and graph.

"After about 2 weeks I saw an easier way to work. $\frac{A}{V} = \frac{6x^2}{x^3} = \frac{6}{x}$ so divide 6 by the number of sides – so 12 sides would be $\frac{1}{2}$. I don't think this graph will ever touch the axis as even a million sides would be $\frac{6}{1000000}$."

Peter's research into calculus

A verbatim report is given here of latter part of a tape recording of a talk which Mr J. Aitchison (Inspector, City of Nottingham) had with Peter Barnes (aged 11 years) on his approach to calculus via gradients. In the first part of the interview, Peter had described class experiences which led to his awareness of the graphs of $y = x$, $y = x^2$ and $y = x^3$. The part reported here is of his own research. Mr Aitchison had previously selected the pages of Peter's work which he wished to discuss and had the relevant tables and/or graphs extracted – labelled *with the numbers of Peter's pages (pages 9 to 15)*. These are reproduced here in context, though not shown as Peter did them on $\frac{1}{10}$ inch graph paper (too space-consuming). Finally, in Peter's language, the progression was from 'gradient of graph' $y = x$, to 'gradient and area beneath' $y = x^2$ then $y = x^3$ – then back to 'area beneath' $y = x$ – which led to the final pattern that evolved for graphs $y = x$, $y = x^2$, $y = x^3$ and $y = x^4$.

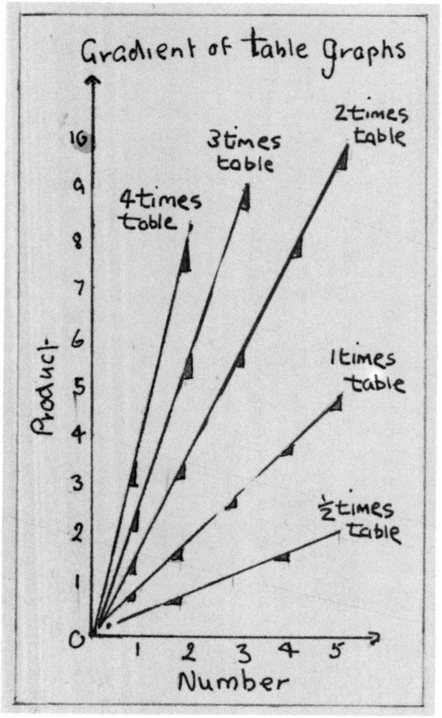

Fig. 8.7 (above) Page 9

Fig. 8.8 (right) Page 10

chart (below)

Times table	Gradient	Angle	
5	5 in 1	79°	$1\frac{1}{2}$°
4	4 in 1	$77\frac{1}{2}$°	$5\frac{1}{2}$°
3	3 in 1	72°	8°
2	2 in 1	64°	9°
1	1 in 1	45°	
$\frac{1}{2}$	1 in 2	$27\frac{1}{2}$°	
$\frac{1}{4}$	1 in 4	15°	
$\frac{1}{8}$	1 in 8	$7\frac{1}{2}$°	

Mr A. *On page 9 you drew these graphs.*

Peter Yes. I then drew the gradients of the different tables separately. I did them for tables 1, 2, 3 and 4 and found the degrees 45°, 64°, 72° and $77\frac{1}{2}$°. I then thought that for $\frac{1}{2}$ times table the gradient would be $22\frac{1}{2}$° as $22\frac{1}{2}$° is half of 45°. I put down $22\frac{1}{2}$° not knowing that this would be wrong, and then I actually got a protractor and found that it was $27\frac{1}{2}$°. With these straight lines the gradient is the same at all points along the graph. I then drew gradients 1 in 4 and 1 in 8 – their angles were 15° and $7\frac{1}{2}$°. I put them in order in the chart.

Mr A. *Now on page 10 I see you have a graph of gradients and their angles.*

Peter Yes, well I drew a graph because I wanted to show in graph form the degrees of different gradients. . . I drew the lines of reference across from the gradients and down to their angles.

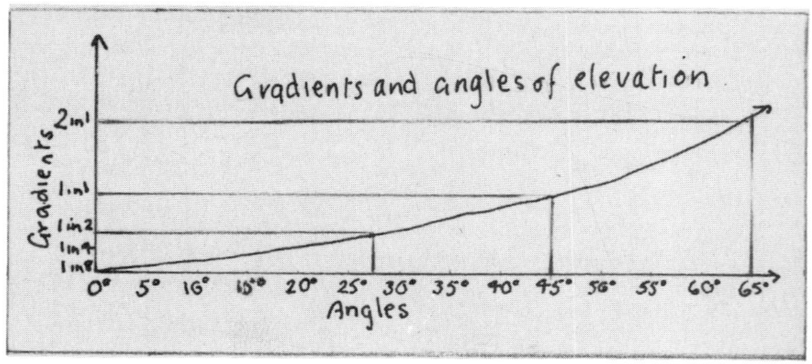

I found that as the gradients increased from 1 in 1 the degrees between them were less – see the graphs get closer. I then drew a very stiff slope with angle of elevation nearly 90°. Could it be 90°? . . . No or the line of slope would be vertical and not a slope. It could be 89.999999° but never 90°.

Mr A. *On page 11 you have drawn graphs of the table of squares.*

Peter Yes, I wanted to find the gradients between the points on this graph. The gradients I found were 1 in 1, 3 in 1, 5 in 1 and 7 in 1. After seeing these numbers I thought they were odd numbers. I wanted to find the gradients 2 in 1, 4 in 1 and 6 in 1. I thought that these gradients would be *at* the points as the ones I had done already were *between* the points.

I then drew another graph of the tables of squares, and put tangents on all the points, and found the gradients . . . I drew the triangles at the different points and I found the gradients 2 in 1, 4 in 1 and 6 in 1, and I also found that the formula was $2x$ because all the gradients were twice the value of x.

Mr A. *On page 12 you have the same graph.*

Fig. 8.9 Page 11

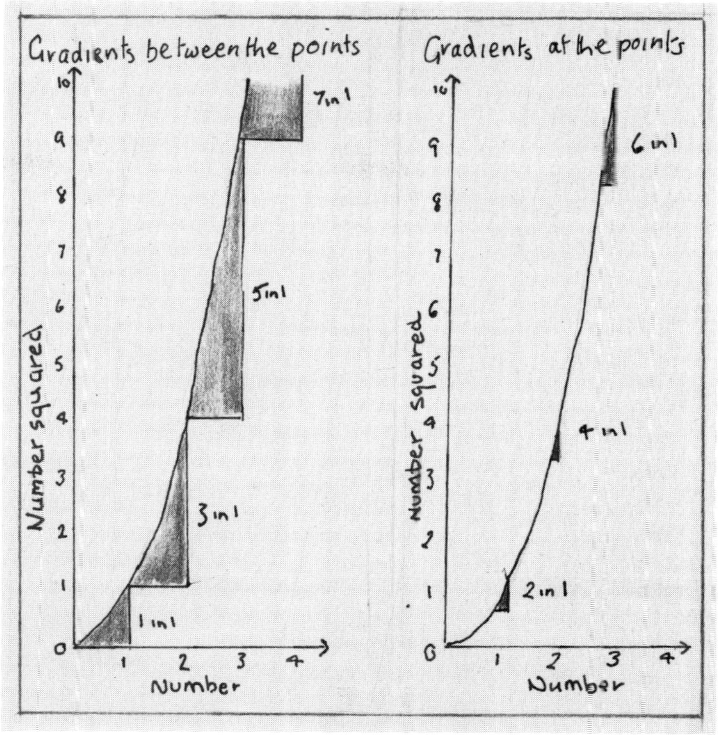

Fig. 8.10 Page 12

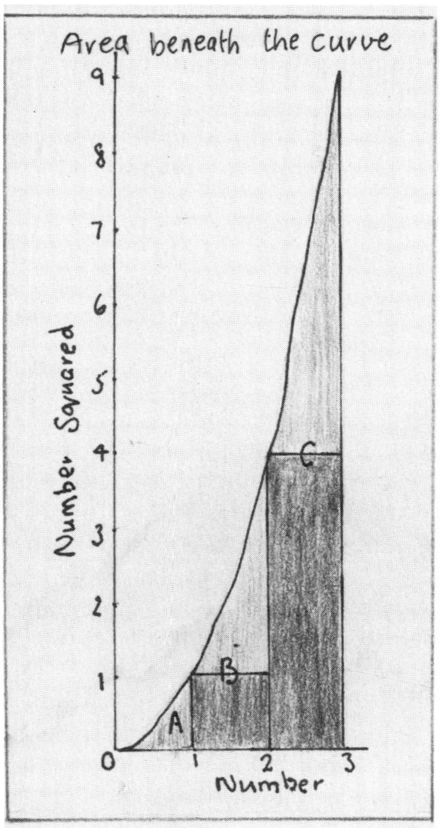

Peter Yes, I wanted to find out really what the areas were beneath the triangles (**Mr A**. *Beneath the curves*). Beneath the curves.

I crossed off the small squares beneath the curve and found that for the section 0 to 1 it was $8\frac{1}{3}$ small units which was in fact $\frac{1}{3}$ of that unit. From the *x* axis of 1 to 2 it was $2\frac{1}{3}$, from 2 to 3 it was $6\frac{1}{3}$ and from 3 to 4 it was $12\frac{1}{3}$ [pointing to the table below].

These numbers have an increase in pattern of 2, 4, 6 – increase by 2. I then wanted to find out what the total would be of these numbers, so I added the first and second sections together, then the first, second and third together, then the first, second, third and fourth together. I got these numbers $2\frac{2}{3}$, 9 and $21\frac{1}{3}$.

Area between	Area
$x=0$ and $x=1$	$\frac{1}{3}$ sq. unit
$x=1$ and $x=2$	$2\frac{1}{3}$ sq. unit
$x=2$ and $x=3$	$6\frac{1}{3}$ sq. unit
$x=3$ and $x=4$	$12\frac{1}{3}$ sq. unit

Area between	Area
$x=0$ and $x=1$	$\frac{1}{3}$ sq. unit
$x=0$ and $x=2$	$2\frac{2}{3}$ sq. unit
$x=0$ and $x=3$	9 sq. unit
$x=0$ and $x=4$	$21\frac{1}{3}$ sq. unit

Fig. 8.11 Page 13

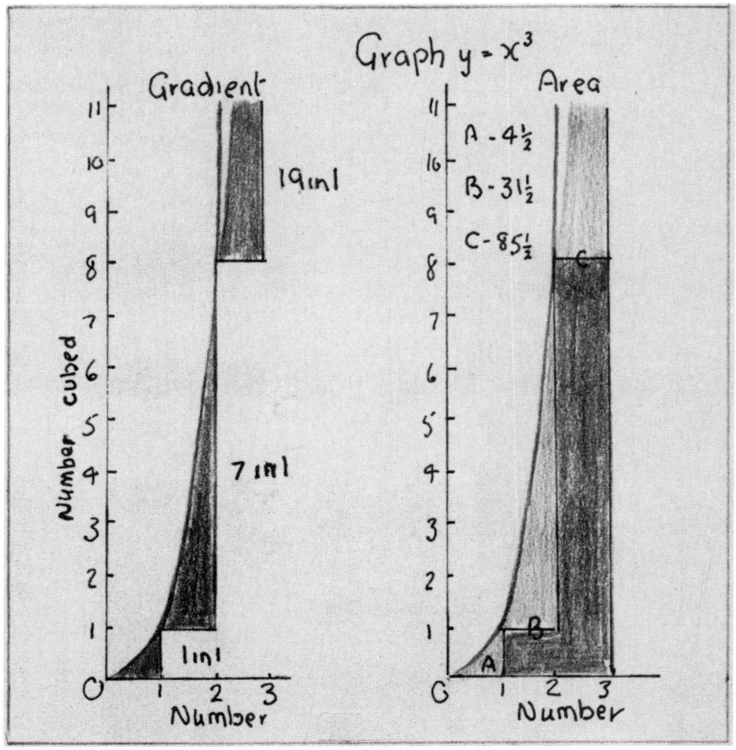

These numbers were . . . no . . . I could see no pattern in them, and to make them whole numbers I multiplied by 3 as the numbers were in thirds. The numbers I got were 8, 27 and 64. These are the cubes of numbers, so the area under the curve is the x number cubed divided by 3[or $x^3/3$]. I then plotted these areas on a graph and found the gradients at the points. The gradients I got were 1 in 1, 4 in 1, 9 in 1, which were the table of square numbers which I had already started with.

Mr A. *Now to page 13 – the graph of $y = x^3$ I see.*

Peter On page 13, I did the same as I did for the table of squares to start with the cubes of numbers. I found the gradients which were 1 in 1, 7 in 1, 19 in 1, and the areas. The areas I found were $4\frac{1}{2}$ small square units, $31\frac{1}{2}$, $85\frac{1}{2}$ and $166\frac{1}{2}$ (by pattern). I found the differences of these numbers, and then the differences again, and the differences of the differences increased by 27, 27, 27 and 27. I then wanted to find the gradients at the different points for this graph, and the formula for doing this. I did this at home for about a week, and tried to find a formula. I guessed it would be $3x$. I found the different gradients at the different points but none of them were quite right, each one was different from the one before. Then we came back to school and Trevor and I tried it. We put the gradients down that we had found, and Trevor saw that the formula should be $3x^2$, and from there we found

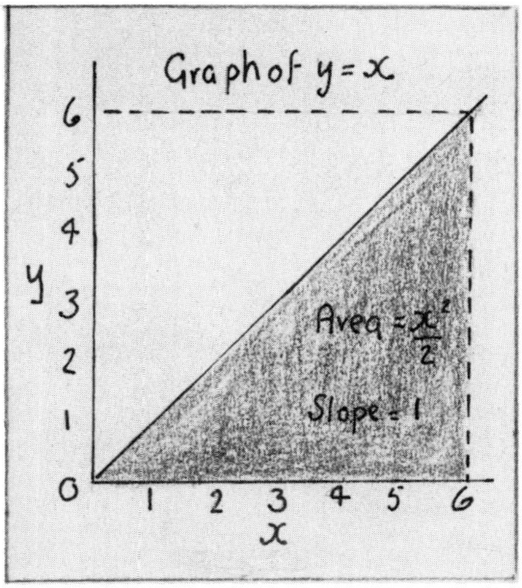

Fig. 8.12 Page 14

out all the other different gradients, and we proved this on a big piece of graph paper on which we could see clearly all the different gradients.

Mr A *Now on page 14 I see you have gone back to the graph $y = x$.*

Peter Yes, Miss Biggs came to school and was seeing us do these different graphs, and she suggested that we do this graph which was $y = x$ which was a straight line. We found how to find the areas under the line which was by squaring x and dividing by 2. We also found the slope equals 1.

Mr A. *I see this is your last page.*

Peter Then on page 15, I put together the facts that I knew.

For the graph $y = x$, the slope is 1 and the area	$\frac{x^2}{2}$
For the graph $y = x^2$, the slope is $2x$ and the area	$\frac{x^3}{3}$
For the graph $y = x^3$, the slope is $3x^2$ and the area	$\frac{x^4}{4}$

Mr A. *But I haven't seen where you found out in your book that the area is* $\frac{x^4}{4}$.

Peter No, you haven't seen it but I guessed that this is right because it follows the pattern of the other areas.

Research-minded pupils

And now to some generalisations about personal tendencies among research-minded pupils of whatever age or sex. I have found that they are somewhat possessive of their research problem, almost akin to writers with their scripts. Suggestions which are offered advisedly are acceptable, but directives are not. On the other hand, a receptive ear can offset any feeling of loneliness and also, in the process, promote clarification. A practical means of meeting this need surfaced in Peter's lone research, when Trevor was recruited as co-researcher. I purposely brought him in when Peter had been chasing $3x$ as the slope for $y = x^3$ for about two weeks. As will be noted, Trevor solved the problem. One proviso is that the helper must have status – no child should act as a stooge. One further tendency should be guarded against. These children should not become so absorbed in the research that they lose other interests. John was an active Scout, Helen was a keen and practical allrounder, and Peter had a healthy interest in cricket. This is good – a child is only a child once.

With regard to the research itself, no conclusions were in mind, as understood in mathematical terminology. John was not motivated to find the rule for factoring the difference of two squares. Helen, though inspired at first with the practical issue of relating sequences to graphs, then turned to interrelationships. Peter had no idea that his research was leading into calculus. When I gave him a copy of *Calculus for Beginners* after his taping, he brought it back next day and said, "Why do books make things that are so easy so hard to follow?" This was food for thought!

Identifying signs

Attitude

Ideas being pursued in the classroom act as spring-boards for pupils with initiative to take off on some track of their own. Signs may well be obliviousness to what is going on around them (even the sound of break-bell), and also writing on scraps of paper which are hurriedly pushed under the desk when these children 'emerge' from their train of thought. It is interesting to note the linguistic/mathematical interaction: these children seem to write with ease on what they think or rethink.

Features of observation and research

There are two main features: a recognition and dependence on pattern and also, often via pattern, an extension to the infinite. With regard to pattern, Paul gives a wonderful example in tracing the pattern of perimeters (page 50), and then allocating the sequences across the multiplication chart (page 51). All three pupils mentioned in this chapter are natural observers and users of pattern. They exemplify the extension beyond the immediate concrete example to what can be envisaged. Relate this to Helen's prognosis that her graph (page 83) would never touch the axis.

Lastly let me mention a practical point. If research-minded pupils are discovered at primary school, it could be most helpful to contact the Principal Teacher of Mathematics in the secondary school when the children move there. An awareness can prove very beneficial both to the pupil and the teacher.

Appendix: Notation (across the age-range)

This part of the text has been left till last because of the intrinsic nature of notation. Systems for expression of numbers are contrived by people, and are just tools furnished to express symbolically the growth of conceptual understanding rather than conceptual understanding itself. The intricacy of a structure of notation extends logically according to need. The following account illustrates the emergence of such a structure.

Two practical aspects will be discussed here: The first is problems inherent in the concept of place value in our common base 10 notation (with a lead into index notation), and the second is the extension to bases other than 10, showing the common structure in bases, from the now much-used base 2 to base 10 inclusive.

Place value and base 10

John, a young visitor to my house, rode round and round it on his small cycle. "I bet your house cost a hundred pounds", he called out as he passed by. "More than that," I threw out to his retreating back. "Then a thousand", he offered dismissively on his next round. "More than that", I cried out as he shot forward again. Next round brought his final bid, "Well a million", he called out conclusively. Who can argue with that as a limit? Subject closed!

Which brings me to an occasion when this was not the case. When I met Brian, he was in tears – on enquiry I found out why. "It's Paul", he said, then added between gulps, "I've been counting five hundred every night in bed till I get to a million, and guess what he said, 'What about it? Then you can go on to a million and one can't you?'" How would you have met that? Which brings me to how a junior class (aged 8–9 years) came to grips with a million.

Making a million

Miss Chambers' class (called 2C) contained the scapegoats of the school. If anything was amiss you could go straight to 2C and stand a good chance of finding the culprit(s). Searching around to give the class a new image, Miss Chambers hit on the idea of making a million. She requisitioned the school stock of very large sheets of $\frac{1}{10}$ inch squared paper (with bold lines marked for inches). The plan was to cut, mount and label 1, 10 (as ten 1s), 100 (as ten 10s), 1000 (as ten 100s) and on to 1 million, section by section. The work was allocated. It was interesting that the class thought they would be finished by playtime! It was fascinating for me, a visitor, to hear them allocate work across groups; indeed at one time all were engaged in producing thousands.

Finally, there, occupying the terrace, was their million with stages leading up to it lined up in order. So possessive were they of their achievement that they organised shifts to guard it from 'snoopers'. The Head, privately warned of course, was escorted to view *their* million. He reacted to their complete satisfaction: amazed and delighted, as indeed he was. He decided that the whole progression should be displayed in the hall, ready for school assembly next morning.

Fig. A.1 How big is a million?

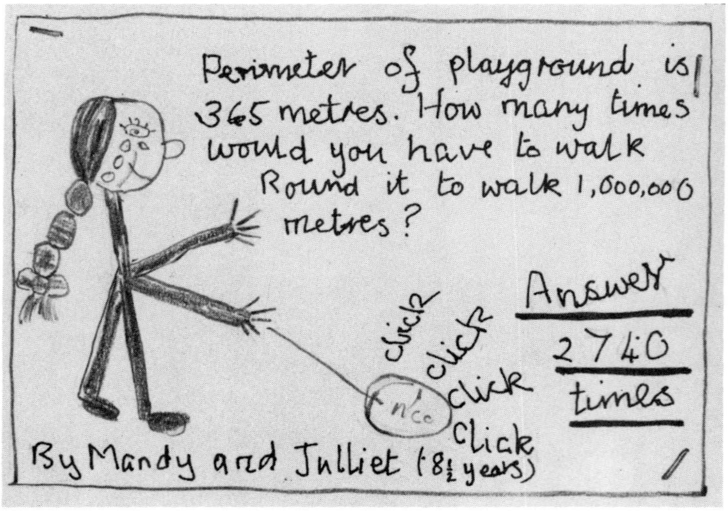

The morning arrived. There was the display under the title *2C's MILLION*. 2C was asked to stand, and one of the children, Jill, was invited to come out and explain. The class then received an ovation from the whole school! Of course, as teachers will surmise, 2C did not become virtuous overnight, but a self-respect had emerged. As for the mathematical repercussion, a quite unforeseen craze for a million swept the school and indeed, through the grapevine, spread to other schools. Fig. A.1 shows the results from one such school.

Index notation and decimals

One secondary teacher of mathematics thought it would be a good idea to let her first-year pupils also make a million. She foresaw that this display, with its stage by stage structure would provide a background for establishing index notation and at the same time revise the function of the decimal point and introduce or revise operations where it is involved.

First, with reference to the display and the structure in Fig. A.2, they built up the chart from 10^0 to 10^6. (Note that to multiply by 10, move a digit to the left; to divide by 10, move a digit to the right. Here is further proof of the senselessness of using the gimmick, "to multiply by ten add nought". The move into negative indices was made realistic through their practical application as illustrated in Table A.2. The chart was completed by the teacher's older pupils to 10^{-3}.

	m	100 th	10 th	th	h	t	u		$\frac{1}{10}$	$\frac{1}{100}$	$\frac{1}{1000}$
10^6	1	0	0	0	0	0	0	.	0	0	0
10^5		1	0	0	0	0	0	.	0	0	0
10^4			1	0	0	0	0	.	0	0	0
10^3				1	0	0	0	.	0	0	0
10^2					1	0	0	.	0	0	0
10^1						1	0		0	0	0
10^0							1	.	0	0	0
10^{-1}							0	.	1	0	0
10^{-2}							0	.	0	1	0
10^{-3}							0	.	0	0	1

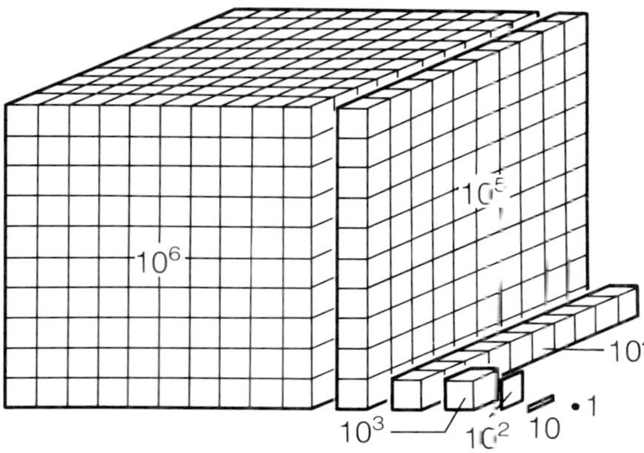

Table A.1 (above)

Fig. A.2 (above right)

Table A.2 (right)

	Money	Length	Mass	Capacity
10^{-1}	10p as £$\frac{1}{10}$ or £0.1	1 dm as $\frac{1}{10}$ m or 0.1m	1 dg as $\frac{1}{10}$ kg or 0.1kg	1 dl as $\frac{1}{10}$ litre or 0.1 litre
10^{-2}	1p as £$\frac{1}{100}$ or £0.01	1 cm as $\frac{1}{100}$ m or 0.01m	1 cg as $\frac{1}{100}$ kg or 0.01kg	1 cl as $\frac{1}{100}$ litre or 0.01 litre
10^{-3}		1 mm as $\frac{1}{1000}$ m or 0.001m	1 g as $\frac{1}{1000}$ kg or 0.001 kg	1 ml as $\frac{1}{1000}$ litre or 0.001 litre

Comparisons between, say, money and length can increase understanding of the function of the decimal point (and provide apparatus) at any age. For example,

£		10p	p		metre		dm	cm
3	.	6	2		3	.	6	2

This is helpful in making operations meaningful. How about using a metre ruler to find change?

68 cm + ☐ cm = 1 metre → Answer 32 cm

68p + ☐ p = £1 → Answer 32p

A boy did this during a film which I made with the B.B.C., to help the interviewer 'understand' change from £1 – nearly overturning their expensive apparatus in an effort to reach a metre ruler!

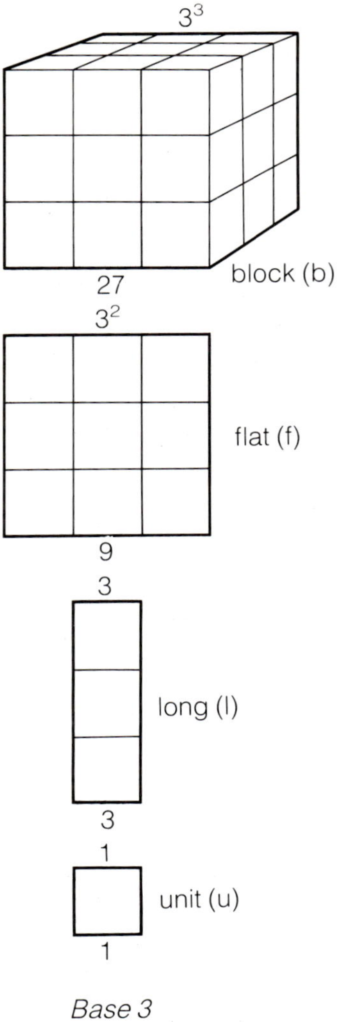

Fig. A.3 (above)

Extension to other bases

I offer here a method I adopted to introduce bases 2 to 10 to a class of 10–11 year old pupils. My aim was to lead up to an understanding of the common structure of bases, with the binary system particularly in mind. I had by me, for reference, sets of Dienes M.A.B. – two of which are shown in Figs. A.3 and A.4. Note the extension from units via longs and flats to blocks (a helpful visual presentation), and also use of index notation.

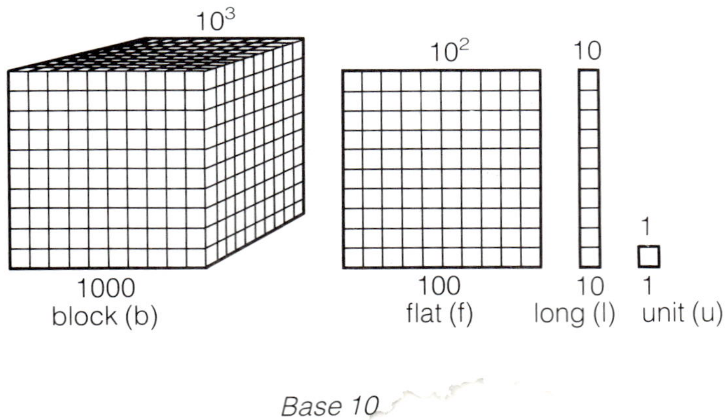

Fig. A.4 (right)

First they investigated bases in common use, as follows.

Number	Base 2 qt pt	Base 3 yd ft
(0)	0	0
(1)	1	1
(2)	1 0	2
(3)	1 1	1 0

and

Base 5: fingers → 1 hand
0,1,2,3,4,10
(as five is 10 in base 5)

Base 7: days → week
0,1,2,3,4,5,6,10
(as seven is 10 in base 7)

Base 10: fingers → pairs of hands
0,1,2,3,4,5,6,7,8,9,10

Table A.3 (right)

Bases

10	9	8	7	6	5	4	3	2
l u	l u	l	l u	l u	l u	l u	l u	l u
0	0	0	0	0	0	0	0	0
1	1	1	1	1	1	1	1	1
2	2	2	2	2	2	2	2	1 0
3	3	3	3	3	3	3	1 0	(1 1)
4	4	4	4	4	4	1 0	⋮	
5	5	5	5	5	1 0	⋮	(2 2)	
6	6	6	6	1 0	⋮	(3 3)		
7	7	7	1 0	⋮	(4 4)			
8	8	1 0	⋮	(5 5)				
9	1 0	⋮	(6 6)					
1 0	⋮	(7 7)						
⋮	(8 8)							
(9 9)								

Table A.4 (below)

Row	Base 10	Base 9	Base 8	Base 7	Base 6	Base 5	Base 4	Base 3	Base 2
(1)	10^2 10 1	9^2 9 1	8^2 8 1	7^2 7 1	6^2 6 1	5^2 5 1	4^2 4 1	3^2 3 1	2^4 2^3 2^2 2 1
(2)	100 10 1	81 9 1	64 8 1	49 7 1	36 6 1	25 5 1	16 4 1	9 3 1	8 4 2 1
(3)	f l u	f l u	f l u	f l u	f l u	f l u	f l u	f l u	b f l u
	0	0	0	0	0	0	0	0	0
	1	1	1	1	1	1	1	1	1
	2	2	2	2	2	2	2	2	1 0
	3	3	3	3	3	3	3	1 0	1 1
	4	4	4	4	4	4	1 0	1 1	1 0 0
	5	5	5	5	5	1 0	1 1	1 2	1 0 1
	6	6	6	6	1 0	1 1	1 2	2 0	1 1 0
	7	7	7	1 0	1 1	1 2	1 3	2 1	1 1 1
	8	8	1 0	1 1	1 2	1 3	2 0	2 2	1 0 0 0
	9	1 0	1 1	1 2	1 3	1 4	2 1	1 0 0	1 0 0 1
	1 0	1 1	1 2	1 3	1 4	2 0	2 2	1 0 1	1 0 1 0
	1 1	1 2	1 3	1 4	1 5	2 1	2 3	1 0 2	1 0 1 1
	1 2	1 3	1 4	1 5	2 0	2 2	3 0	1 1 0	1 1 0 0
	1 3	1 4	1 5	1 6	2 1	2 3	3 1	1 1 1	1 1 0 1
	1 4	1 5	1 6	2 0	2 2	2 4	3 2	1 1 2	1 1 1 0
	1 5	1 6	1 7	2 1	2 3	3 0	3 3	1 2 0	1 1 1 1
	1 6	1 7	2 0	2 2	2 4	3 1	1 0 0	1 2 1	1 0 0 0 0

They used the idea of transfer to fill in Table A.3. This enabled them to reach one zero in each base and to find the limit for each one (bracketed here) before flats were needed.

As this was a very lively class, I thought I would try out an idea I had used with secondary pupils. I gave each group a framework for Table A.4, a share each of bases 2, 3 and 4 Dienes M.A.B., and suggested they fill in to 10 as before, and then continue into the next columns. (2^2, 2^3, 3^2, 4^2) using flats and blocks. They liked that.

Then I drew the class together again to look at the framework of the chart, and we filled in their units and longs. With material for other bases on hand, we discussed when flats would take over from longs in bases 2, 3, 4 and on. Suddenly one group went into a heated exchange. We waited, then the leader explained, "There's no need to think hard like we are doing. Just look at the number in row (2) across. All you have to do is to repeat a base's numbers that number of times. Do you understand?" They didn't, and I was groping. A kindly girl took over. "See *base 2* uses 0 and 1, for longs it repeats two 0s and two 1s, flats four 0s and four 1s, and blocks eight 0s and eight 1s (the numbers in row 2). *Base 3* uses 0, 1, 2, for longs it repeats *3* of each and flats *9* of each." Light dawned for some of us. Of course when base 10 is written 0, 1, 2, 3, 4, 5, 6, 7, 8, 9 is repeated 10 times for longs and 100 times for flats. We all clapped them – those who understood and those who did not. (Note that the blanks at the top of each column count as 0s.)

The binary system

Here is a practical way to establish the binary system: line up and number 'models' as in Fig. A.5. Select a caller of numbers 0 to 15. The rest of the class watch and 'advise'. The action needed is an arm up by a model if their number is required. For example 1 needs A only, 2 needs B only, 3 needs B and A, 4 needs C only, on to 15 which needs D, C, B and A.
A rhythm emerges in line with the pattern (see the columns in Table A.4).
A (units): down/up repeatedly, 0,1 repeated.
B (longs): twice down/twice up repeatedly, 0,0,1,1 repeated.
C (flats): four times down/four times up repeatedly, 0,0,0,0,1,1,1,1 repeated.

Conclusion

This section on bases may well have substantiated an opinion that has grown throughout the book that the approach leans towards what is commonly described as 'new mathematics'. The emphasis on 'relatedness', or 'ordered pairs' or even the

Fig. A.5

basic idea of 'sets' may well have fostered the conclusion. I quote here two opinions that offer an appraisal of mathematical education in this context.

A spontaneous and gradual construction of mathematical structures exists as a function of the development of intelligence – such structures are much closer to those being used in 'modern' mathematics than those being used in 'traditional' mathematics. (Piaget)

There is a popular distinction between 'traditional' and 'new' methods in the teaching of mathematics, but this terminology is extremely unfortunate. The methods called 'new' have been advocated for many years, by many teachers and educational writers. The methods have aimed at independent thinking, the understanding of principles and the ability to tackle fresh related problems. It has always been recognised that the practical realisation of these aims is difficult. The debate is not so much over the desirability of these aims, as over their feasibility given the available teaching force . . . In England there is no one thing which can be called 'new' or 'modern' mathematics. If any school or institution claim to be doing something with such a name, only by looking at the details is it possible to learn what they understand by the name.
(H.M.I. Appraisal of Mathematics in 'Maintained Schools of England').

My own training in mathematics consisted of a progression from chapter to chapter of a textbook. It was only when I began to teach that I realised that hopping from idea to idea was time-wasting, both for me and my pupils. It took time and thought first to insert my own experience and then the children's into a structure based on relatedness. My purpose in writing this book is to describe children's reactions when taught within this framework. I hope that such a presentation can offer a similar experience to an inservice course where teachers, even those diffident about their own mathematics, realise that their knowledge only needs reorientating. Take the teacher responsible for the biological examples in Chapter 2. Quite suddenly during a session she broke a momentary silence by exclaiming, "The penny has just dropped! All I need to do is to adjust what I know as I do in biology." I could not myself have achieved a more positive impact. To me, by the way, it is immaterial which name is given to my approach. If pressed to specify I would describe it as a realistic one, influenced as it is by two seemingly opposite factors: the invariant logicality of the subject itself and the varying aptitudes of children.